The Information Audit

The Information Audit

and information asset register – a practitioner's guide for the Freedom of Information Act.

Chris Higson &
Sebastian Nokes

Rivington

Rivington Publishing Ltd.

London • Wellington • Melbourne • Geneva

RIVINGTON PUBLISHING LTD
Head Office:
22 The Avenue
Kew Gardens
Richmond
TW9 2AJ
Great Britain

www.InformationValue.com   0207 588 5544

Published by Rivington Publishing Ltd., London.
First published in Great Britain 2004 © Rivington Publishing Ltd.
Email: info@InformationValue.com

The rights of professor Chris Higson and Sebastian Nokes to be identified as
the authors of this work have been asserted by them in accordance with the
Copyright, Design and Patents Act 1988.

ISBN 1 84578 000 0

Many of the designations used by manufacturers and sellers to distinguish
their products and services are claimed as trademarks. The publisher
acknowledges all trademarks.

British Library Cataloguing in Publication Data
A catalogue record for this book is available from the British Library.

Library of Congress Cataloging in Publication Data
Applied for.

Typeset in-house by Rivington Publishing Ltd.
It is Rivington's policy to use paper and materials from sustainable sources.

ACKNOWLEDGEMENTS

A large number of people have assisted in the thinking that has gone into the Melbourne information audit – they have assisted either with ideas fundamental to its design or by trusting us to apply the audit to their organizations in various stages of its evolution. We would like to thank in particular Andrew Munro, JP Rangaswami, Diana Burton, Roy Varughese, Dave Best, Catherine Griffiths, Peter Robin, Ian Major, Clarence Meredith, Tony Bolton, Dillon Dhanecha, Tegwen Wallace, Kennedy Fraser, Caroline d'Cruz and Gwenda Sippins. Dr Jade Prince, Patrick Smith, David Tulloch (in Wellington), our colleagues at Aldersgate Partners LLP have also each put significant effort into developing the ideas and tools, and also in the editing and preparation of this book, ensuring that it is a finished product – Jade putting sterling work into Chapter 4 in particular. We would also like to thank Chris Booton for his hospitality in Melbourne, where this book was largely written and where some of the necessary research was done. Last but absolutely not least, we wish to thank Brigadier (Ret'd) Mike Stone and his fantastic team at BTopenaccess, our home-from-home.

COLOPHON

This book was created using Adobe® InDesign® CS. It was written in Microsoft® Word and IBM® ViaVoice™. The computers used were an Apple® Macintosh G4 Powerbook™ 17" and various 15" machines. We used the idea processors Inspiration® from Inspiration Software® and IdeaFisher™ from Idea Fisher Systems Inc.

TABLE OF CONTENTS

INTRODUCTION

Most organizations have a reasonably good understanding of their physical and financial assets: what assets they possess, what condition they are in, what they cost and what they are worth. They want to know this because from hundreds or even thousands of years of historical experience managers know that such an understanding is a precondition to sound management; they may also have to know this because the law might require them to account for these assets. But the same has not applied to information assets. Many organizations do not even known what information assets they have and do not have systems to account for these assets. However, this is changing. In the information economy, organizations are realising that their information assets are among their most valuable resources and that there is an enormous payoff to building and nurturing them. In the public sector, the law is rapidly pushing organizations in this direction in any case.

From January 2005, the Freedom of Information Act enables individuals to demand from UK public sector organizations disclosure of the information in their possession. Public sector organizations cannot comply until, at the very minimum, they have a register of what information they hold and can access that information readily. In the private sector it is one of the top priorities of many of the biggest and most respected companies to understand their information assets better. It is one of the priorities of Lord Brown of the oil company BP, for example[1].

The information audit is the key first step in creating a register of the organization's information and the core process in maintaining and exploiting that register thereafter. This book is a practical guide to the Melbourne information audit. But first we give a small amount of background. Readers who wish to jump straight in to doing an audit should go to chapter 3.

The approach we describe to information auditing in this book, the Melbourne methodology, is more powerful, and simpler, than existing methods. The power of the information audit methodology we describe arises from thinking about information as an asset. Just like the organization's tangible assets, its stock of information has continuing value, but it is costly, requires investment and maintenance, and it depreciates over time. We need to record its location, understand who uses it, and we need to ensure its proper stewardship.

Of course, there are some respects in which information is quite different in nature from the organization's other assets. First, information is an intangible asset and shares features with some of the organization's other intangible assets such as intellectual property, brand and reputation. These assets tend to be diffuse in nature, which can make it hard to identify their cost and can make them hard to value. Secondly, the sheer novelty of thinking of information as an asset like traditional assets. Thirdly, the feature that makes people struggle with accounting for information is its apparent extreme granularity. After all, the quantity of data that most organizations nowadays possess, or might possess, is enormous. How can we possibly bring order to this? Again, asset-thinking provides the solution. We show that the key is to think about information assets, rather than data or records, which means aggregating information to as high level as is sensible. This means thinking about information in terms of its purpose and in terms of its value to the user.

A car provides an excellent analogy. There are many thousands of parts in a car and a mechanic might look at a car and think about spark plugs, bearings, wheel nuts. But the owner sees a car and thinks about its fitness for purpose, its condition, and ultimately its value to him as the user. We show that thinking about information assets in this way is transforming for an organization. Shifting away from a focus on data and records greatly simplifies the information audit process while focusing attention on what really matters. What matters is how information is used, its value to the organization, the adequacy of the organization's information stock, the potential gaps in information provision, and so forth.

An information audit is the vital first step in applying asset thinking to information. The context and goals of an information audit will determine the nature of the work that needs to be undertaken. There are three main contexts for an information audit.

> *To support a programme of process improvement.* For example, information audits as preparation for the installation of an EDRM system.

> *To improve the organization's understanding and management of its information resources.* More ambitiously, the information audit

may be undertaken with the explicit goal of developing a knowledge management strategy.

To meet a legal or regulatory requirement. An example is an information audit undertaken in the context of the Freedom of Information Act or the Data Protection Act. Financial audits are also of this sort.

These goals are not mutually exclusive and an audit project will often be trying to meet more than one of these goals simultaneously.

With or without regulatory compulsion, organizations in both the private and public sectors are recognising the need to start accounting for information. Brands provide a good example of how resource allocation in branded goods companies radically shifted once those firms recognized brands as the unit for accounting and started to develop ways of valuing them. A similar process is under way, though at an earlier stage, for human capital. We believe that public sector organizations will reap great benefits from accounting for their information assets.

WHAT IS INFORMATION?

Much of the time, people use the words 'data' and 'information' in a way that is interchangeable. For instance, in the sentences "go and collect the data we need" or "have we got the relevant information?" either word could be used. But it is helpful to some people to draw a distinction between data and information in the following way:

Data are the basic particles: data are "thing[s] given or granted; something known or assumed as a fact, and made the basis of reasoning or calculation; assumption[s] or [premises] from which inferences are drawn...." (*Oxford English Dictionary*, 2nd. Edition).

Information is valuable data. That is, information is data that is relevant or useful. So the idea of information is inseparable from the idea of value.

Information has value to the extent that it is relevant or useful. What does this mean? Faced with a complex world and the need to make decisions and initiate actions, humans develop mental models or frameworks to help them structure and understand the world. Information is useful when it validates or invalidates one or more of these working models, or helps us form new models.

The knowledge of an individual or an organization is the stock of models about its world, the working practices based on those models, and the information to support those models and practices that it holds.

Information systems and information technology define the processes and systems that collect, process, store and deliver information. Since the amount of data available to an organization is potentially unlimited, what should it collect? The measure of information is its usefulness, and to make rational investment decisions about information organizations need to be able to measure information's usefulness. To do this we need to understand the way in which the organization using the information measures its own welfare or wealth. For a firm, the working hypothesis is that the goal is to maximize the value of the stream of profits the firm is expected to earn in the future. So the value of a piece of information is the amount it adds to a firm's value. It follows that information relevance is synonymous with information value. We will use the word 'value' instead of 'relevance' from now on. In fact, information value is a more powerful idea than information relevance because value is priced relevance.

---

[1]   Nokes, S. Personal Communication.

Chapter 1

INFORMATION AS AN ASSET

The rewards to seeing information and knowledge as assets have been enormous for the organizations that have done this. An information audit is the first step in implementing asset-thinking for information. Equally, in preparation for the first information audit or when the auditor is familiarising themself with the audit tool, the key is to become comfortable with the idea of information as an asset. This chapter develops those ideas.

An information audit is a systematic review and assessment of an organization's information assets and of its information management processes. It helps in building an information audit methodology to see the parallels between an information audit and a traditional financial audit. It is no surprise that these are related since financial information is simply a part, a rather well organized and well understood part, of the entirety of the organization's information.

However, how does information fit with conventional notions of an asset? The determining feature of an asset from an economic perspective is its longevity. In accounting, an asset is the right or access to future economic benefits that is controlled by the firm as a result of past transactions or events. So expenditure creates an asset when it is expected to yield economic benefit in more than one time period.

Information has a stock and a flow aspect in a
way that physical assets usually do not, or at
least do not to the same degree. This is an idea
with some history, for example: "We could ...
distinguish between the stock of knowledge
and the flow of information."[1] Individual items
of information are frequently transitory; they
are specific to a place and time. A stock of
information, an information resource, usually
only has longevity if it is replenished with a
flow of new information. The extent to which
the stock will need to be replenished and the
frequency of updating determine the cost of
information and depend very much on context.
In financial markets information resources are
commonly updated daily, or by the minute. To
pursue the analogy with physical assets, a stock
of information can be viewed as an asset that
may require continuous maintenance to preserve
its functionality.

Information is most efficiently thought of in
aggregate and indeed at as high a level of
aggregation as possible. So the information asset
may comprise many separate items or atoms
of information. For example, in a personnel
database, the useful unit for analysis may be the
personnel record of one individual, comprising
as it does much data from many sources.

INFORMATION CLASSES

The first step in valuing information is the
identification of a decision. Having identified
the decision, we identify the domain of
information needed to make the decision.

We showed earlier that information is useful
when it has the potential to guide action or

behaviour. In practice, therefore, the measure of information is its relevance to a decision or decisions, and the measure of the value of information will be the benefit resulting from the decision. Sometimes information is used to inform ourselves about a situation and is often called "background information." But even in those cases, the ultimate aim is to make a decision – why do we need background information? Ultimately, we need it as background to a decision.

Consider the decision "Should the organization invest in Project P?" The domain may span the following pieces of information:
-   the best estimate of the cost of Project P and the risk and sources of error in that estimate;
-   the best estimate of the benefit of the project and the risk and sources of error in that estimate; and
-   the financial characteristics of the organization that relate to project finance, which are chiefly the risk-free rate of interest, the risk premium to be used for the type of project under consideration, and any constraints on payback and total investment size.

Because of the particular nature of information as an asset the next step is to aggregate the information into information classes or information products.

Describing information as an asset is a readily understandable use of the word. We will also use the slightly more encompassing word 'resource' interchangeably with asset. However, how does information fit with the conventional understanding of an asset? The determining feature of an asset from an economic perspective is its longevity. As we have said in accounting, an asset is 'the right or access to future economic benefits that are controlled by the firm as a result of past transactions or events'. So expenditure creates an asset when it is expected to yield economic benefit in more than one time period.

Information has a stock and a flow aspect in a way that physical assets usually do not, or at least do not to the same degree. Individual items of information are frequently they are specific to a place and time. A stock of knowledge usually only has longevity if it is replenished with a flow of new information. The extent to which the stock will need to be and the frequency of updating determine the cost of information and depend very much on context. In financial markets information resources are commonly updated daily or by the minute. To pursue the analogy with physical assets, a stock of information is perhaps best thought of as knowledge and can be viewed as an asset that may require continuous maintenance to preserve its functionality.

The analyst should identify a parsimonious set of information classes or information products as the basis for analysis. In this process he groups information that from a user perspective is part of the same resource. Information can be grouped with other information into an information class when it is highly correlated in use or when one piece of information dominates or subsumes the other.

FINANCIAL AUDIT

The starting point for a financial audit is the organization's balance sheet, which contains an inventory of its assets. The assets that traditional accounting systems recognise as assets include tangible assets such as property and machines, and stocks of raw materials and finished goods, and financial claims such as debts from other firms and cash in the bank. The auditor checks that those assets exist and puts a financial value on them.

The balance sheet describes the *stock* of assets but we also want to know how assets flow in and out of the organization. For a firm, the income statement and the cash flow statement both try to describe this flow, one in terms of the flow of costs and revenues, the other in terms of the flow of cash. We expect the organization to have a system in place for the stewardship of its assets and a system of internal control containing checks and balances to ensure that assets are not damaged or lost by accident or deliberately. We also expect an organization to have an accounting system that measures the stocks and flows of assets.

In summary, an audit involves:
-   Inventory. The construction or checking of an inventory of information assets;
-   Transactions. Charting the way in which information flows through the organization;
-   Valuation. Assigning a financial value to the asset.
-   Stewardship. Reviewing the organization's systems for the stewardship and management of its information assets.

The amount of work the auditor has to do depends on how good the organization's systems are. If the organization has adequate accounting and internal control systems, the auditors will do a random check of the assets but will spend most of their time checking the systems. Large organizations have their own internal auditors to do this, in which case the job of the external auditor involves checking the internal audit systems. At the other extreme, in small organizations there will frequently be no real accounting system at all and the auditor's job is also to be the accountant producing the basic financial statements.

INFORMATION AUDIT

All of the above comments describe an information audit in which the same principles are applied to a new asset class – information. At its most basic, an information audit is an assessment of:
- What information exists in an organization
- The purpose of the assets, or what they are used for
- Its quality, that is its degree of fitness for that purpose
- The sufficiency of the information, that is, does the organization have access to all the information it needs, and if not, what are the gaps?
- The risks inhering in the assets
- The structure of the information assets
- The value of the assets
- The sources, controls over, and uses of the assets
- How effectively the assets are being used
- How efficiently the assets are being used
- Where and in what format are the assets? and
- How are they accessed?

But if we are thinking about all of an
organization's information assets the potential
domain is much larger; containing at one end
of the spectrum, financial and non-financial
data recorded in physical and electronic form
and, at the other end, what are frequently called
knowledge assets: the manuals and procedures
that capture the organization's knowledge
and, perhaps, the tacit knowledge held by
individuals. Somewhere in the middle, and
rapidly growing in importance in the modern
age, is information such as that contained in
the organization's e-mail traffic or in voice
recordings from call centres.

KNOWLEDGE AND HUMAN CAPITAL

Where does knowledge reside? Knowledge may
reside in the consciousness of employees, or
may even be unconscious or tacit knowledge. It
is communicated actively through training and
passively by observation and work experience,
'on-the-job training'. It may be formalized, which
is to say, externalized in systems and manuals.
A related and troublesome question is, does
organizational knowledge truly rest with the
organization rather than with individuals, and,
if the latter, can knowledge truly be said to be
organizational? The balance of power in control
of knowledge differs from firm to firm and
context to context.

If the ability to create a nexus of knowledge
workers will be important for production where
workers are engaged on projects that require
the different skills of different people. Pursuing
the example of university, this may take place
in a research centre. The individual needs his

colleagues. Individually, his knowledge may have little value and it may only gain value in combination with the knowledge of others. If the individual cannot work alone then his only alternative to working in the current team is to join another team.

In commercial research and development organizations, projects may have a much longer history (and more accumulated shared knowledge) and require much greater infrastructure. This shifts the balance of power over knowledge strongly toward the organization. Hence the relative success of research and development organizations in retaining key workers in, for example, the pharmaceutical sector. A contrast would be equity researchers in stockbroking firms. Here there is relatively little unique infrastructure, the infrastructure that is required is a commodity. Knowledge is specialised and is retained at the level of the individual analyst or the sector group. Firms have been relatively unsuccessful in creating an organization-wide knowledge architecture. As a consequence, individual analysts and teams of analysts move with great regularity.

---

[1] Strijdom, P.D.F. "The Economics of Information" in Boettke, P.J. (Ed.) *The Elgar Companion to Austrian Economics*. Aldershot (Elgar Publishing): 1994. ISBN 1-85278-581-0

Chapter 2

RATIONALE FOR THE AUDIT

There are two reasons for a public authority to have an information audit. First, the audit will provide significant business benefits, and this is a sufficient reason to conduct the information audit. But secondly, for public authorities, the requirement under the Freedom of Information Act also requires it.

The business benefits of an information audit are that it will:
– reduce operational risks by increasing the quality of information held by the organization, because better information means better, less risky, decisions.
– reduce the cost of managing the organization's information by eliminating surplus holdings of information, eliminating nugatory reconciliation effort, and identifying areas where new technology or techniques can be applied to reduce costs of holding information.
– increase efficiency by increasing the availability or utility of information to business processes.
– support other business improvement initiatives, particularly in knowledge management, and improve capability and competency.

The experience of IBM, British Telecom and a number of other private sector corporations shows that benefits identified by the information audit will be significant. IBM conducted an exercise similar to an information audit in the mid 1990s which enabled it to reduce office space significantly by reducing the amount of filing cabinets worldwide. The result was a multi-million dollar annual cash saving.

How are these business benefits achieved? The greatest benefits will derive from being able to understand the organization's information assets and from aligning information assets to business needs at the highest level. In financial management it is well known that having a complete view of cash management is essential to achieve optimal use of cash resources, to minimize risks, and to maximize strategic agility. It is exactly the same with information management.

What does this mean in terms of specifics, from an information audit? It means being able to answer questions such as:
-   How many duplicate sets of information do we hold, and can we eliminate the excess holdings?
-   What are our most valuable information assets? Are we maintaining them and protecting them to a degree appropriate to their value?
-   What are the opportunities to rationalize our holdings of information by adopting one of several similar sets of information as the corporate standard?
-   Where are there material opportunities to increase our recovery of costs associated with information assets?
-   What revenue opportunities are we missing?

The information audit model described in this book, the Melbourne information audit, enables us to answer such questions by analyzing our information assets. The audit produces a list of information assets, that is the information asset register, and for each asset a list of its attributes. (Annex B shows a copy of the review template in its initial form.)

This means that many questions can be answered, for example:
– What proportion of the information assets that we hold for regulatory purposes and no other reason are held as paper documents?
– What are our most shared assets?
– What proportion of our assets are held in office accommodation but are accessed very infrequently?

THE UNDERLYING PRINCIPLE OF THE MELBOURNE INFORMATION AUDIT

The information audit is based on the principle that information is a key asset to the organization and as such needs to be managed properly. Key steps in managing information properly entail making decisions about the acquisition, retention, use and disposal of information. The problem in making these decisions is to balance competing investment opportunities within the objectives of the organization. This problem is the same as the problem of managing human resources, financial resources, equipment resources or property resources. In all those other areas the audit is a well-developed tool for assisting in such decision-making, and the information audit is the equivalent of such tools for managing information.

The information audit answers seven key questions about the information assets held by an organization, namely:

- What are the assets?
- Why do we have them (or what are they used for)?
- Are they of sufficient quality?
- Do we have the right assets and are we using them well?
- Do we have enough of them?
- Where are they and how do we get hold of them when we need them?
- How much is each asset worth?

HOW INFORMATION IS USED IN ORGANIZATIONS

The classical theory of information is associated with a vision of economics and of economic actors, which was mechanistic and drew heavily on paradigms from physics and engineering. In a control context, the organization already has a model of how the world works or how we want it to work, a production plan, a marketing plan, and a financial budget. Control is only problematic because of uncertainty. The external environment and the performance of the factors of production are not fully predictable. If the system displays entropy, in the sense of a tendency to decay into chaos, then uncertainty will tend to grow without control. Information alerts us to deviation from plan or to aspects of the plan that were incomplete. In response we may change actions or modify or complete the plan.

Shannon[1] was working within this control
framework and is usually represented as the
leading exponent of this classical view. He
took an engineer's perspective on information.
Information reduced uncertainty by embodying
data which permits one to choose between
competing hypotheses. Shannon anticipated
data processing by noting that the key motive for
translating information into different media was
change its space-time properties so as to enable
its reproduction at a different time or a different
place.

Information for decision-making, for instance
information used in decision support in
financial services, frequently follows the control
paradigm. The decision model is largely
identified, but with some parameters left
variable and to be determined on a case-by-case
basis using relevant information. Pricing of
financial instruments is a good example of the
use of information to reduce uncertainty.

These control settings all contain the potential for
learning, so one should beware of creating a false
dichotomy. But by learning we are particularly
interested in the use of information to inform
and to trigger strategic shifts, to bring about a
change in the organization's and individuals'
understanding of the world and to support
continuous innovation.

The complex adaptive system paradigm is better
suited to a turbulent and interrelated world. It
offers a more exciting but challenging vision of
the role of information. While in the classical
paradigm information simply holds back the
flood of disorder to a greater or lesser extent, in

the adaptive or biological paradigm organisms and organizations that can learn and adapt can create new order. Its ability to support learning is key to the modern theory of information.

All organizations need information for control, for adaptation and for learning; information for efficiency *versus* information for flexibility. The balance between information for control and information for learning and information for flexibility depends on the context, on the location of the activity within the firm, and on the competitive environment of the firm. This view, this balance, of the different uses of information in an organization is also seen in process modelling, for instance the IDEF0 modelling methodology, which makes the same distinctions between different uses of information.

Most fundamentally, the organization's need for information for control, and for information for adaptation and learning, will depend on the organization's context. For organizations in a static setting the main concern will be information to control existing operations. Such organizations will face relatively little change in their technology and in demand, and relatively little competitive threat. An example of such a firm might be a water utility in the pre-privatization world. For firms in a dynamic or turbulent setting where technology is rapidly changing or the marketplace is highly contested, information for adaptation and learning will be paramount.

According to Macdonald[2], "Organizations find information much, much easier to use for efficiency than for flexibility.... Information systems rather than information transactions are required.... The information is thoroughly familiar to the organization and generally neatly codified. The channels through which it flows replicate the hierarchical structure of the organization and pose no threat to structure and control. This is the sort of information with which information technology deals most readily. It facilitates the type of information transfer that is often associated with the larger organization, with mass production and with routine work organization."

A template for the structure of the information resource in an organization (Figure 2.1) depicts generically the ways in which information is used by organizations and provides a template against which to assess the informational needs and informational scope in any organization we are looking at.

In a control context, we already have our model of how the world works or how we want it to work, a production plan, a marketing plan, and a financial budget. Control is only problematic because of uncertainty; the external environment and the performance of the factors of production are not fully predictable. If the system displays entropy, in the sense of a tendency to decay into chaos, then uncertainty will tend to grow without control. We use information to alert us to deviation from plan or to complete aspects of the plan that were incomplete. In response we may either change actions or modify the plan.

INFORMATION FOR LEARNING, ADAPTATION AND FLEXIBILITY

More recently, a paradigm has emerged which, in some ways, could not be more different from the classical information paradigm. We will call this the modern theory of information. This theory has its roots in the complex adaptive systems (CAS) models developed in biology[3]. In the mechanical paradigm of classical economics, actors, be they employees or firms, are distinct yet homogeneous entities. They respond to their environment but cannot change it. In contrast, we now see that economic entities form part of an ecosystem containing individuals and firms which are both specialised and diverse but mutually dependant. In the modern world even the boundaries of the entity are blurred. Individuals and firms operate through relationships, networks and alliances which transcend formal definitions of the entity. They interact with their environment, responding to it, but also changing it by their actions, and changed by it. In a turbulent and rapidly changing world, successful firms need organizational knowledge that contains models not just of how their world works but of how the world might be. Their information systems must yield the information flow to support this modelling.

The information balance shifts from learning to control as one moves down the organizational hierarchy, as the balance of managers' responsibilities shifts from strategy to implementation. But again, there is a danger in generalization – in a learning organization learning takes place at all levels.

Most fundamentally the organization's need

for information for control, and for information for adaptation and learning, will depend on the organization's context. For organizations in a static setting the main concern will be information to control existing operations. Such organizations will face relatively little change in their technology and in demand, and relatively little competitive threat. An example of such an organization might be a water utility in the pre-privatization world. For organizations in a dynamic or turbulent setting, where technology is rapidly changing or the marketplace is highly contested, information for adaptation and learning will be paramount.

The case of SABRE [4]demonstrates how investments in information that started with the objective of organizational efficiency could easily lead to the strategic use of information for organizational flexibility. The use of information by certain major airlines in the US enabled them to strengthen their competitive advantage even after deregulation of the industry in 1978. Airline deregulation did not turn out as expected, partly because the uneven control of information in a very information intensive industry created strong barriers to entry.

The SABRE reservation system came on stream in 1964. "…deregulation produced surprises, many of them springing from the growing strategic use of information by some airlines. The deregulation of the US airline industry should have brought increased competition. Instead, it allowed companies to make increasingly strategic use of information (for example, in its computer reservation systems, yield management systems, and frequent flyer programmes), which meant that use of

Fig. 2.1
How Information is used within organization

Behaviour (that is decisions and actions)	Information Environment (that is decisions and actions)		
	Financial Information	Internal Non-financial Information	External Information*
MICRO Purchasing, input acquisition. Production: converting inputs to outputs. Process control & improvement.	Revenue Cost accounting. Product accounting. Cost allocations. Revenue recognition.	Project experience. Quality management. Employee satisfaction & work-life balance.	Process benchmarking. New process innovation. Competitor's prices and products.
TACTICAL Product decisions (what price, what product / market).	Product profitability	Customer satisfaction. Employee knowledge. Organizational learning.	Market share. Demand. Customer satisfaction.
RESOURCE ALLOCATION Invest / disinvest. Financial control.	Business performance	Employee knowledge.	Rivals' performance. Public expectations.
STRATEGIC	Options architecture Understand the strategic options.	Organizational performance.	Opportunities, risks, regulation, oversight, threats, legal and governance.

* (both financial & non-financial)

information often determined competitive advantage. The development of the US airline industry since regulation illustrates this transition from the use of information for efficiency to the use of information for the flexibility that strategy demands." [5]

IS INFORMATION A SOURCE OF COMPETITIVE OR ORGANIZATIONAL ADVANTAGE?

Possession of a resource creates value if that resource confers competitive or organizational advantage. We measure the competitive advantage of a firm in terms of its ability to earn a return greater than its investors' required return. The value added of a resource is the incremental return it brings to the firm, expressed as a present value. The concept of advantage carries over perfectly to the non-market sector of the economy. Now, a resource confers organizational advantage when it brings sustainable benefit in excess of its cost. In perfectly competitive market places, all resources, including information, are commodities. It is always a good discipline for the analyst to have a presumption that markets are competitive and, *per contra*, to need persuading that they are not. So the central question when assessing the value of information is when information should simply be viewed as a commodity, and *per contra*, when and how information creates value.

In the description of SABRE, above, the strategic use of information, its use for adaptation and learning, was also associated with the creation of competitive advantage. But these are not synonymous. For instance, in strenuously competitive industries, firms may be forced to learn and adapt continuously merely to survive, while never creating competitive advantage. On the other hand, we can conceive of a situation where the possession of production control and efficiency technology not possessed by others might confer competitive advantage. An example of the sort of context in which information might create value would be a proprietary trading system in an active fund management or hedge fund context. In this setting, analysts may have found ways of selecting and combining financial data to generate profitable investment strategies. This is a poignant example because research has shown quite clearly that it is very difficult to create competitive advantage in fund management. Those who are failing to create any competitive advantage are likely to be destroying value when they invest in expensive proprietary information systems where much cheaper commodity information systems are available. IT is often the back-bone of a financial services business. As a result, one often hears the argument that although the bank has not established any competitive advantage and is not earning superior returns, nonetheless, the IT system is valuable because without it the bank would not exist. An expensive IT system is the price the bank pays for staying in the game. Of course, the point may be precisely that in economic terms there is no reason for the bank to exist.

A TEMPLATE FOR THE STRUCTURE OF THE INFORMATION RESOURCE IN AN ORGANIZATION

Figure 2.1 depicts the ways in which information is used by organizations generically and provides a template against which to assess the informational needs and informational scope in organizations. The template shows an organization during a snapshot in time and describes what information is collected, where it is collected from and how it is used by the organization.

The model looks at an organization along two dimensions - its behaviour and its information environment. Behaviour is defined as the company's decisions and actions, from the micro level through to the tactical, resource allocation and strategic levels. These decisions and actions are made by all employees of the organization, from line workers to the management board. The information environment contains financial and non-financial data, collected both internally and externally. The financial information is very familiar and is the most consistently and regularly collected information in all types of organizations. The internal and external non-financial information, on the other hand, ranges from hard statistical data to softer qualitative data.

The financial and non-financial information have corresponding behavioural counterparts, different levels of micro, tactical, resource allocation and strategic decisions. Some types of information, such as employee knowledge, have applications across many levels. The granularity characteristics and aggregation states differ across the levels and the model. The upper

28

left corner of the information chart typically contains small bits of control data which support micro level decision-making, whereas the lower right corner of the information environment represents strategic decision-making based on high-level aggregated externally derived data.

[1] C. E. Shannon. "A mathematical theory of communication". *Bell System Technical Journal*, vol. 27, pp. 379-423 and 623-656, July and October, 1948.

[2] S. Macdonald, "Learning to change: An information perspective on learning in the organization", *Organization Science*, 6, 2, 1995, pp.557-68.

[3] Boisot and Cohen (2000) provide an excellent review and comparison of the classical and modern theories.

[4] Semi Automated Business Research Environment. SABRE is now one of the largest airline ticketing, booking and billing systems.

Chapter 3

HOW TO RUN AN INFORMATION AUDIT

This chapter is a manual of how to set up and run an information audit. It assumes some understanding of the concept of an audit, and some familiarity with how organizations work. Readers who just want to get on with the audit may start at this chapter.

OVERVIEW OF THE INFORMATION AUDIT PROCESS

There are fourteen distinct steps in conducting an information audit, but these can be grouped into five overall tasks as follows:

- A. Prologue – familiarization.
- B. Project administration.
- C. Audit administration.
- D. Audit kickoff.
- E. Complete of the audit.

These tasks are a sequence. The first of these five tasks is separate and must be completed before the four main tasks (B - E above), and is no more than a few hours at most to ensure that whoever is managing the audit is sufficiently familiar with the audit tool in order to be effective in the remaining four phases. These four phases are the main part of the audit. The audit may be decomposed into the full fourteen tasks as follows:

A. Prologue - familiarization

    1. Ensure that the core audit management team understands the tool.

B. Project administration

    2. Decide on the purpose of the audit.
    3. Agree a mandate or charter for the audit.
    4. Determine the scope of the audit, and list the audit areas.
    5. Identify the auditees – who are the managers of the audit areas? (or their designees).
    6. Determine, in general terms, the skills and capabilities of the auditees.

C. Audit administration

    7. Select the audit tool.
    8. Finalize the audit team.
    9. Finalize the audit plan.

D. Audit kickoff

    10. Brief the auditees.
    11. Initiate the audit.

E. Complete the audit

    12. Monitor the audit and manage by exceptions.
    13. Identify, exploit and communicate quick wins.
    14. Close the audit.

In this chapter we will go through each step of the audit. In the next chapter the audit tool is described heading by heading. Apart possibly from step 1, *ensure that the core audit management team understands the tool,* the greatest use of the audit tool in the fourteen steps of the audit is in step 11, *initiate the audit*; additionally, it will be a significant feature of steps 10 and 13, *brief the auditees* and *identify, exploit and communicate quick wins* respectively. It may also feature significantly in steps 2 to 9, that is throughout the project administration and audit administration phases. Before using this chapter to plan and run an audit, therefore, the people (or the person) managing the information audit must be familiar with the tool, that is the first step or the prologue to the audit must be completed.

TERMINOLOGY USED IN THE INFORMATION AUDIT

Before describing the audit step-by-step, some terms used in that description should be defined.

Information. We do not define information. Those who want or need information audits will already have their own definitions of the word, albeit implicit and quite possibly approximate. There is little value, given the aims of this book, in spending time on the matter. However, we can say that information is at the very least the same as data, and for most users of the term means something more than mere data.

Information Assets. An information asset is an asset which is information, as the term implies. The question, then, is what is an asset? An asset is a thing which creates value, or, which is in fact the same, has the potential to create value. The word derives from *ad satis*, meaning towards sufficiency. As managers we are accustomed to thinking of physical assets, most typically plant and equipment, that is vehicles, computer hardware and buildings, as assets. We are also increasingly used to thinking of people as assets, our human assets we might say. And there is an increasing trend to think in terms of intangible assets, of which examples include brands, reputations, patents, contracts, contacts and so on. Information can be an intangible asset. This is a very old idea indeed. The idea - the information – that seven blasts of the trumpet after a period of silence would destroy the walls of Jericho is a very early example of the value of an information asset. In this example the asset also had huge negative value for those defending Jericho, and assets with a negative value are often called liabilities, but for simplicity in this book we will treat all information assets, whether having positive or negative value, as being termed assets. Indeed, one of the most compelling reasons for undertaking an information audit is to determine whether your organization's information assets are assets or liabilities.

Information Audit. At its most basic, an information audit is an assessment of:
- what information exists in an organization,
- the purpose of the assets, or what they are used for,
- its quality, that is its degree of fitness for that purpose,
- the sufficiency of the information, that is, does the organization have access to all the information it needs, and if not, what are the gaps?
- The risks inhering in the assets.

In addition, an information audit may also analyze or assess:
- the structure of the information assets,
- the value of the assets,

- the sources, controls over, and uses of the assets,
- how effectively the assets are being used,
- how efficiently the assets are being used,
- where and in what format are the assets? and
- how are they accessed?.

The information audit can also be a way of understanding how data is imported in to, used by, produced by, and moved through a company. Some commentators emphasize one of these roles over the others, and often it is the flow of information which is emphasized, in order to identify gaps or discontinuities in an organization's data flows.

The information audit is also designed to meet the requirements of the section 46 Code of Practice to the UK's Freedom of Information Act 2000, which states that every public authority subject to the Act should "Conduct an information survey or record audit."

Information Inventory. An information inventory is a list of the information assets held. The most frequent use of an information inventory in this book is in the context of the information audit, and therefore at the level of the audit area. The term is also commonly applied at the level of an organization as a whole, a constituent department, division or directorate within the organization, or a business unit or function or a desk.

Information Audit Manager, Audit Manager.
An information audit, even a small one, will in practice need a manager. It may also have a sponsor or a person to whom the manager reports, but there will be one person who has

operational or day-to-day responsibility for ensuring that the audit happens and assuring its integrity. This person is called the 'information audit manager', or the 'audit manager' for short.

Information Audit Sponsor, Audit Sponsor. The senior executive with responsibility for the information audit. The audit manager reports to the audit sponsor for the purposes of the audit project. The sponsor will not personally manage the audit on a day-to-day basis, for that is the role of the audit manager. The sponsor oversees the audit and is accountable to the board of directors or the management committee of the organization within which the audit is being conducted for the use of resources by the audit and for the quality and value of the results.

Audit Management Team. In a large information audit the task of managing or overseeing the audit is often more than one person can manage, and so the audit manager may be assisted by a team, part time or full time. In some audits this team may be one other person, or the team may be many people. In some audits the team is made up of sub-audit managers. In other cases they may be filling a training role. All of these possibilities are included under the term 'audit management team'.

Audit Area. The audit area is that part of the organization within which an audit or part of an audit is being conducted. The boundaries to an audit area are thus organizational boundaries.

Auditees are the managers of the audit areas, and – depending on the context – their designates.

Audit Methodology. The audit methodology is the

one described in this book, which is also called the Melbourne methodology[1].

Audit tool. The audit tool is the software tool by means of which the audit methodology is implemented. This is either a spreadsheet or a database. (The Melbourne methodology and the headings and structure of the audit template given in this book is copyright © 2004 Rivington Ltd, and permission should be sought before using the methodology in an IT system or PC.)

TABLE 3.1 - Example of part of a completed audit of one asset

INFORMATION ASSET	Location	Narrative description of Asset	Name of file series of main folder	Who owns this information asset? (A - E)
Records of regulatory review cases	Headquarters, Room A107 (in Legal & Compliance Department)	These are the findings of cases investigated by the Regulator.	OFREG Cases	A

*

With what other information assets is this asset closely associated? How?	Golden Source	Does the asset derive more than 50% from material in the public domain?	Structure (S, T, U)	In what format is the information? (P,E,D,T,C,X,O)
None	No	Yes	Unstructured or semi structured	P-A4

*

If paper, what factors would affect replacing it with an electronic version?	With what business process is the information associated?	How is it associated?	Is there a description or map of the process?	What is the source of the information? From where do you get it?
None – they could be scanned into electronic form.	Statutory duty, quality assurance and performance measurement	It is an output of the regulatory investigation process	Complaints procedure booklet describes part of the process, this may need to be brought up to date. Legislation (1989 Act et seq) specifies some of the process.	1. Complainant. 2. The regulator. 3. The Organization's business unit at issue. 4. Legal Svcs.

* The table represents a single row in a spreadsheet. To fit it on the page, it has been chopped into three parts and stacked.

A. PROLOGUE - FAMILIARIZATION

1. Ensure that the core audit management team understands the tool.

(If the audit manager and, where there is one, the audit team, are already familiar with the Melbourne Information Audit Tool, this step can be missed.)

The familiarization phase of the audit ensures that the core audit management team understands the tool, or at the very least that the manager of the audit understands the tool. Unless the people planning and leading the audit have a minimal understanding of the tool, they will not be effective in planning nor managing the audit. It takes very little time to reach the necessary minimal level of familiarity – in the order of a day or a half day.

The audit managers must use the tool themselves before directing others to use it. They must familiarize themselves with the audit. The first step in doing this is to select an information asset to audit. How should someone unfamiliar with the process of an information audit select an information asset? The ideal asset for this purpose will be from the operational or business part of the audit area rather than from the administrative or support part. That is to say, the asset will be a piece of information connected to what the audit area does, its function, rather than being connected to the administration of the function. For example, if the audit area is a strategic planning team, then strategic plans, financial analyses and industry surveys are business assets, whereas the HR records and holiday and sickness logs of the members of the strategic planning team are administrative information assets. The ideal asset will not be too large; for familiarization purposes it is best to practice on an asset that is manageably small.

The output of this familiarization exercise will be a completed spreadsheet containing the audit results of one information asset. The spreadsheet template (that is, the spreadsheet version of the audit tool) will have one completed row with the name of the information asset on the left, after which in each column will be the values of the attributes of that asset. Table 3.1 is an example of how some of the result of this familiarization exercise might look – it is the first ten columns of the Melbourne audit template when completed for one particular information asset; this is the spreadsheet implementation of the audit tool and each column is used to record one aspect of the information assets, each row being one asset's attributes. (The rest of the columns are not shown for reasons of space, but examples are given in Chapter 4). This output is of course not the main output, but rather is a by-product of the main output of this stage. The result is that the audit manager (or audit team) will have achieved at least a minimum level of skill and experience necessary to use the tool to plan and manage the information audit.

The next chapter describes in detail each attribute of information captured by the standard version of the audit tool. However, most of the key information in that chapter also appears in comment boxes in the spreadsheet version of the information audit tool, which means that the audit manager who is not yet familiar with the tool may be able to complete this first step, familiarization, without reading the next chapter, or, at most skim-reading that chapter should suffice.

To familiarize themself with the audit tool the audit manager should select an information asset to audit and then complete one row of the audit tool.

How should someone unfamiliar with the tool, and moreover unfamiliar with the process of an information audit and its terminology, select an information asset? The first point to make in answering this question is to delimit the kind of information asset most suitable for the purposes of familiarization.

So we have specified that the asset should be a business asset rather than an administrative one and that it should be manageably small, but how to identify an information asset? The easiest way is to list some of the main activities undertaken by the person who is the manager of the audit in their role within the audit area. What are the main things they do in their job? Taking the example of the strategic planning team, a person who is a member of this team might come up with the following list:

- Analyze cost data from internal functions,
- Analyze industry sector,
- Create report for the board of directors,
- Produce annual and quarterly strategic plan.

"Things that they do" is another way of saying "process," so this is a list of business processes. If there exists a list of business processes for the audit manager's area, this can also be used. Business processes, typically, have information

Table 3.2 – Example of lists of information assets associated with processes in a hypothetical strategic planning function.

Process	Information Asset
Analyze cost data from internal functions.	– Cost reports from financial controllers. – Management reports from internal functions. – Comparative data from other organizations or industry bodies – Audit reports. – Completed reports (i.e. written by the strategic planning team).
Analyse industry sector.	– Industry body reports. – Internal reports on dealing with the sector. – Regulatory reports (ombudsman, etc) on the sector. – Independent research reports on the industry. – Newspaper articles. – Completed reports on industry sectors (i.e. written by the strategic planning team).
Create report for the board of directors.	– Reports for the board of directors. – Emails from the board giving guidance on what reports are required. – Research material for use in writing the reports. – Case files relating to issues of concern to the board.
Produce annual and quarterly strategic plan.	– Annual strategic plan (i.e. written by the strategic planning team). – Quarterly updates to the strategic plan. – Comparative data from external databases. – Financial reports and accounts (internal) for previous periods.

assets as inputs and outputs, and also as controls. So once you have a list of business processes it should be a simple matter to identify the associated information assets. Taking the list of processes in the example above we can postulate some likely information assets associated with each:

The point of this slightly lengthy hypothetical example is to show that in practice identifying information assets is very easy if one approaches the task from a process perceptive. For the purpose of familiarization it does not matter which information asset is chosen, although as we have said it helps if it is manageably small. It is also sensible to select one that is readily to hand and in a convenient format.

Having selected an information asset, the next and only remaining thing to do is to audit the asset. To do this open the spreadsheet version of the tool, enter the name of the asset in the first column and work across the rest of the columns for that row, answering the audit questions. Most of the questions are straightforward, for example: "Location - Which room is it in (if paper); from which PCs or terminals can it be accessed (if electronic)?" Enter the answer into the spreadsheet. For some questions the answer is narrative (that is, free text), for others the answer must be selected from a list of options. For example, the answer to the question "Who owns this information asset?" must be one of A, B, C, D, E, where

"A" means that audit area owns the information; "B" means that the information is owned by the same organization, that is the organization

(company or public authority) of which the audit
area is a part;
"C" means that a supplier owns the information;
"D" means that some other party not a supplier
of the organization carrying out the audit owns
the information;
"E" means that it is in the public domain.

For the purposes of familiarization, and in
practice, in most cases in the audit itself, those
completing the spreadsheet or database should
not spend too long if a few columns are difficult
to answer, it is better to leave them blank and
move on to the next question.

Familiarization is a very simple process and does
not take too long, typically 30 to 45 minutes once
the asset has been selected.

Familiarization provides the audit manager
with two advantages necessary for running a
successful and useful audit. First, it is vital that
the audit manager should be familiar with the
audit tool. Secondly, the issues involved in
conducting an audit will vary from organization
to organization. It will be the responsibility
of the audit manager to ensure consistency
across all audit areas. The audit manager must
be familiar with the tool in order that these
issues and how they apply to the organization
in question can be addressed efficiently
and effectively. Let us give some examples
to illustrate the importance audit manager
familiarity:

Example 1:   How should people in a large,
multi-site organization answer "Location
- Which room is the asset in?" Even if there
are room numbers for every room in the

organization, how will different sites be identified? And if there are no room numbers, how will rooms be uniquely identified? This is not a difficult problem to solve, but the chosen solution needs to be applied consistently if the result of the audit is to have maximum value. The risk is that left to their own devices the audit areas will each use a different approach to question.

Example 2: The meaning of the term "owner," as in "Who owns this information asset?" Is there a standard definition in your organization? If so, ensure that it is applied to the information audit. If not, ensure that this term is applied consistently across the audit, that is create a definition which suits your organization and apply it to the audit.

B. PROJECT ADMINISTRATION

Another term for what is meant here by "audit administration" is "project management", if the information audit were to be considered as a project. The activities to be performed under this heading are not core activities within the information audit, but they are essential to performing an audit successfully, and also to doing so effectively and efficiently. We do not believe, unlike some authors of manuals for information audits, that these activities are what the information audit is all about. They should not be the main focus of audit activities. We mention this because there is a risk that if project management activities are regarded as the main audit activities, the opportunity created by a successful information audit for making the organization as a whole more efficient and effective will be missed entirely. Certainly, the project management activities are vital, but they should not be the main focus of effort.

2. *Decide on the purpose of the audit.*

The organization in which the information audit is to be performed should agree a short statement of purpose.

An information audit, whatever the methodology used, is a substantial effort. Why are we doing it? If we are not clear about this, then misdirection of effort and resources will result in the audit not achieving its goal.

The purpose of the audit must be defined in a written statement. The statement can be as short as a single sentence, but should be no more than a paragraph or two and definitely no more than a page. As with the familiarization stage, the more important output of this step is an intangible one, with all key stakeholders of the audit having a common vision of purpose and benefits of the audit to the organization.

Who does this? Who should decide on the purpose of the audit? In one sense, all stakeholders should. However, in practice it is rare that all stakeholders will meet and decide this. Instead it is usual that the audit manager and the audit sponsor, having been briefed to a large degree already on information audits, will write the statement of purpose (or the manager drafts it and the sponsor approves it). It is then circulated, when appropriate, to the stakeholders.

The reasons for carrying out an information audit are regulatory compliance, systems implementation planning, business process re-engineering and business improvement. Let us look at these in turn.

Regulatory compliance

- To comply with the UK's Freedom of Information Acts (or overseas equivalents), and in particular with the section 46 Code of Practice of the 2000 Act, which stipulates that public authorities should "conduct an information survey or record audit." (The Melbourne Information Audit, which is the subject of this manual, meets the requirements of the "information survey" in the Code of Practice.)

- To comply with the UK's Data Protection Act (or overseas equivalents).

- To comply with the Environmental Information Regulations (or overseas equivalents).

Systems implementation planning

To evaluate the requirements of, or business case for, or to prepare for the implementation of:

- an electronic documents and records management system (EDRMS).

- some other workflow system.

- disaster recovery or business continuity systems, as it relates to holdings of documents and records.

- Intellectual property control and yield management systems.

- Customer relationship or customer interaction management systems.

Business process re-engineering

Most business process re-engineering initiatives fail. One of the reasons is that the re-engineering plan fails to appreciate the value of a few key pieces of information and the way that those pieces are used in critical business process, that is the way that they create value in those processes. For example, one of the (many) reasons that the new London Air Traffic Control at Swanwick, Hampshire, was very late and over budget was that the designers of the re-engineered air traffic control system tried to arrange all the buttons on a controller's screen elegantly ("making them into pretty patterns" as one experienced Royal Air Force air traffic control officer said[2]). These people had insufficient experience of air traffic control and did not appreciate that response times for most people are slightly faster for objects in the left field of vision than in the right field of vision. Therefore, the most mission-critical buttons should be on the left-hand side of the controllers' panels. The designers failed to understand that a couple of hundredths of a second of response time was a significant factor. It may not be for most businesses, but air traffic controllers deal with aircraft often moving towards each other at a combined speed of a thousand kilometres per hour, and a fraction of a second is the difference between life and death. An information audit conducted according to the Melbourne method would have identified the importance of this issue and could have saved the UK taxpayer millions of pounds in wasted re-engineering effort, instead focusing effort according to the value of the information.

Conducting an information audit for the purpose of planning business process re-engineering can materially reduce the risk and cost of the re-engineering initiative.

Business improvement

Business improvement means one of three things: increasing effectiveness, increasing efficiency (which is typically cost reduction) or reducing risk. Business improvement normally refers to the improvement of existing business processes rather than a fundamental re-engineering effort, but the principles of how an information audit adds value to business improvement are the same as those for business process re-engineering, and the example above for business process re-engineering applies also in respect of business improvement projects.

Examples of written statements of audit purposes.

As stated above, the output of this step in the audit process is a written statement of the purpose of an audit. We provide two examples below, both from real information audits conducted in the UK.

3. *Agree a mandate or charter for the audit.*

This step is optional. If it will be useful in the context of a particular organization then it ought to be used, but if not, provided that the audit management team is experienced in managing projects (and if they lack experience in information auditing, experience of managing projects of a kind that is new to them) then this step is probably best dropped.

48

Table 3.3 – statement of purpose from a commercial company

The information audit will answer seven key questions about the information assets held by our organization, namely:

- What are the assets?
- Why do we have them (or what are they used for)?
- Are they of sufficient quality?
- Do we have the right assets and do we have enough of them?
- Are we using them well?
- Where are they and how do we get hold of them when we need them?
- Who knows most about the information?

Table 3.4 – statement of purpose from a public authority

The aim of this information audit is to:

- Meet the Freedom of Information Act requirement for an audit,
- Provide input suitable for use in any review of the efficiency of information handling,
- Assist in aligning information assets with the corporate objectives.

In project management, a mandate or charter is the formal statement of the aims of a project and the authority by which it is authorised, and frequently it also gives a high level indication of the approach to be taken, who will manage and sponsor the project, and the rationale for the project. Ideally the chief executive or head of the organization will sign the charter and it will be sent out in their name to ensure that everyone in the organization understands that the project is the will of the highest[3].

The rationale for having a charter is that it can increase the probability of success of a project, in this case the information audit project, and reduce the cost. Project charters tend to be more valuable for projects that occur in large organizations and involve a large proportion of the organization. This is because, compared to small organizations, it is large ones (and especially large projects within them) where having an explicit statement of support and of clear aims and benefits is likely to most reduce the risk of a project; in a small organization all its members are much more likely to know from informal sources that the project is a priority for the chief executive or head of the organization.

So what is a charter? What should the output of this process look like? A charter is essentially the next extension in terms of detail of the statement of purpose. It includes the statement of purpose, but also gives the rationale for having settled on that purpose, and may also give some indication of the approach to be taken and name the project management team. An example of a project charter for an information audit is given in Table 3.5.

Table 3.5 – Example of a project charter for an information audit*.

INFORMATION AUDIT PROJECT CHARTER

What is the aim?
The aim of this information audit is to:
- Identify sources of high risk in our information holdings or our approach to managing those holdings, so that we can improve risk management.
- Rationalize our holding of information by not less than 30% in terms of volume (paper pages and MB of data), without reducing efficiency or effectiveness.
- Prepare to align information holdings with the departmental mission.
- Comply with the Freedom of Information Act's requirement for an information review.

Key deliverables & dates
The project starts immediately and is due to end on 17 September. This is a very tight deadline, but the organization expects everyone involved, at all levels, to do everything possible to meet this deadline, as we do not intend to allow an extension.

1.   By 30/7/04, a plan for an information audit, including names of "Lead Officers" and "Link Officers" from each function.
2.   By 6/8/04, the first set of trial information audit results into the database from at least 40 of the functions.
3.   By 13/8/04, narrative audit reports in the standard form from all those functions that met the 6/8 deadline, and exception reports from the heads of all other functions together with a revised timetable.
4.   By 3/9/04, the completed set of information audit entries into the database.
5.   By 17/9/04, the final audit report and database.

How? (Approach)
This project will be managed to our standard project management methodology (i.e. PRINCE2 in the Western area and PMBOK in the Eastern area.) The approach to the information audit will be as per the Melbourne methodology, details of which will be provided in due course, and which has already been used successfully by a number of UK public authorities and private sector companies.

---

* *We have just stated that the project charter will include the statement of purpose. This is true, in that it should. Note that the example that we reproduce here of a project charter is not from either of the organizations from which the statements of purpose were quoted in the preceding text.*

Table 3.5 (Cont'd)

Who?
The project will be under the overall direction of Helga Spragg, the Deputy Chief
Executive, and will be project managed by Johnny Thruster, of the Strategic Planning
Department. The Steering Committee will comprise all heads of department plus
Lloyd George-Orwell, Director of Information , John Locke, Head of Knowledge, and
Dredd Halsbury, our external legal adviser.

Each function will appoint an audit liaison officer, and as a group these will be
coordinated and administered by Ayn Rand, our Human Resources director.

Why we are doing it?
The recent public enquiry which covered some key areas of our operations identified
a number of critical vulnerabilities in our existing approach to information
management and retention. In addition we face an imminent regulatory imperative,
in the form of FOI. So the immediate reason is that it is a regulatory necessity.
However, the information audit will also address or enable to be addressed a
number of deficiencies in our processes and information assets that have been
identified over recent years by all heads of department, and where we have analysed
the business case for this type of activity, we have found that it is highly likely to
give cost benefits and to improve effectiveness.

Brody Seer
Director-General
1/6/04

Drafting the mandate or charter should not take long, an hour or two, or half a day at the most even for a large audit. What may take longer in a large organization is the review and editing process to ensure that everyone is happy with it. Ideally, as we have said, the chief executive, chairman or head of the organization should sign the charter and the notice announcing the audit should come from them, in order to invest the audit with the maximum momentum and authority. So they need to be happy with each word, and it is almost certain that they will want to circulate it to their direct reports and possibly the next level of reports below for comment before it is formally sent out.

When the charter is ready, send it to everyone in the organization. These days this will typically be by email, but in 2004 there are still many organizations, especially in the public sector, where a significant proportion of staff who will be critical to an information audit may not have access to email. Some alternative means, usually the good old-fashioned paper memo, should be used to convey the message to these people. The charter should definitely be sent to everyone who will be assisting with the audit, and their management chain. It is recommended that it is sent to everyone in all audit areas, and it may be advisable to send it to everyone in the whole organization. If it is decided to send it only to those who will be involved in the audit, then it cannot be sent out until the end of step 5 of the 14-step information audit process, which is described below, because it is only in that step that those who will be involved are identified – this is a reason for sending it to all staff, because it can then be sent without delay, thereby maintaining the momentum of the project.

4. Determine the scope of the audit, and list the audit areas.

There are two dimensions to determining the scope of the audit, and it is necessary to determine the scope of the audit before it is possible to list the audit areas. One dimension is whether the whole organization should be audited, and if not, which parts should and should not be included. The other dimension is down to what level of the organization should the audit go, or, put another way, what should be the granularity of the audit? The information audit is not only a powerful tool, it is also adaptable and widely applicable in scope. A three day audit covering only the highest level of the organization will yield at least as much value per man-day as will an audit conducted at the lowest level of the organization, even though these are two absolute extreme opposites of scope.

In a large multi-divisional organization with ten thousand or more staff, it may be decided to audit at the divisional level and no lower. In public sector organizations that are preparing for or improving their compliance with the Freedom of Information Act, it is normal to audit at the level of the function or desk or team, or whatever the lowest level of the organization is. When using an audit to prepare for business process re-engineering or to implement a digital information and records management system, then it is more normal to audit at the level that corresponds to a level at which the re-engineering or implementation is being done.

When selecting the level at which the audit is to be done there are two further factors to consider. First, you may wish to evolve the audit so that it covers progressively lower levels of the organization, so that the organization learns about the audit and is better able to manage the volume of audit work that accrues by auditing at the lower level. Secondly, consider the lowest physical unit of audit for paper record. This should usually be – experience suggests[5] – either the room or the filing cabinet; there is usually little value is descending below this level. Naturally, the practicality and feasibility of a scoping decision should be checked before its promulgation.

Write down the decision on scope, stating explicitly the scope in the two dimensions – should the whole organization be audited, or if not, which parts; and dimension is down to what level of the organization should the audit go. This becomes the scope statement. An example of the statement of scope is given at Table 3.6.

TABLE   3.6

A written scope statement is mainly for the benefit of the audit manager and their team as part of basic project management discipline. The statement of scope should be agreed with the audit sponsor. It may also be used in the audit planning document, if there is to be one, and in the audit report.

5. Identify the auditees – who are the managers of the audit areas? (or their designees)

This step identifies, by name, the individuals who manage the audit areas. The information audit project needs to know who they are because these people are vital to executing the audit successfully, and so communicating with them is essential. The output of this step of the audit process is a list of names. This will of course require that all audit areas have been identified, which has been done in the previous step, setting the scope of the audit.

6. *Determine, in general terms, the skills and capabilities of the auditees.*

The purpose of determining the skills and capabilities of the auditees is to allow effective planning of the audit. The suggestion is not to interview or examine the auditees, but for the audit manager or sponsor, in the basis of their knowledge of the organization, to think through carefully what skills capabilities the auditees have relative to those required of them in the kind of audit being planned. If the average auditee is an accountant or an engineer or a Physics PhD, they are likely to have quite different capabilities in carrying out an audit than the average auditee who left school at 16 and has been promoted up the support staff line management function. A large organization may have both extremes of auditee. This is also a factor to consider if an organization is importing an audit model that worked previously in another organization. The output of this step is simply that the audit manager and sponsor should have a common understanding of the likely average capability and its variance. They should discuss the matter between themselves, although it is probably unnecessary to produce any documentation or record.

Table 3.6 – Example of scope statement

SCOPE OF THE INFORMATION AUDIT

This pilot of the information audit at the UK XYZ Agency will cover two parts of the Agency; the Engineering Services Department and the Environmental Performance Department. Each of these is designated an "audit area" for the purposes of this pilot.

The pilot will review the following six information assets:

Engineering Services Department
- Cases for continued operation of facility.
- Accident and sickness reports.
- Performance and productivity monitoring of the Manifold Workshop (regulator's inspection results, schedule and annual report).

Environmental Performance Department
- Liquid waste discharge data (paper copy).
- Liquid waste discharge data (e-copy).
- Solid waste record cards.

With respect to the attributes of the information assets to be reviewed, the scope of this pilot is given by the review template, shown attached [– not shown in this example, but was the spreadsheet version of the Melbourne Information Audit Tool.]

Isaac Liebniz
Deputy CEO
31 March

C. AUDIT ADMINISTRATION

7. Select the audit tool.

If no decision has yet been made on what audit tool or methodology to use, this is the right stage in the process at which to do it. Often it will be the case that from the start the pre-supposition has been that a particular tool will be used, but at other times no particular tool will have been selected, or the organization may be assuming – implicitly or otherwise – that it will make up its own tool as it goes along. The reason that this is the right stage in the process to select the tool is that this is the first point at which there are firm answers to all the preconditions for selecting a tool, namely – What is the purpose of the audit? What is the scope of the audit? Who will be involved in the audit and what are their skills and experience?

If using the Melbourne Information Audit Methodology, then this is the time to consider whether to use the database version, the web version or the spreadsheet version of the MIAMY tool. Many organizations tend to start with the spreadsheet version for a pilot stage of the audit project, and then move to the web or database version once any desirable modifications to the standard audit template resulting from the pilot have been agreed.

8. Finalize the audit team.

The audit management team will manage and drive forward to a successful completion the information audit. Every project needs project management, and at the very least the team will be the sponsor and the project manager. (It is very rare, except in the smallest organizations, that they will be the same person.) However, in an organization of any size the project manager is likely to need some assistance (apart from the sponsor's input) to give the project a reasonable chance of success.

The output of this step in the information audit process is a list of names of people who will form the audit team, and the consents of their line managers (if required) to them being part of the audit team. Note that being a member of the team is not necessarily a full time role. Often, most of the members of a team are taking on the role as very much a part time additional duty. For example, in the information audit for a public authority of approximately 4,000 people, the audit team comprised a sponsor, an audit manager, an audit helpdesk, and two subject matter experts (one to cover the organization's IT, the other to be the expert on the organization's structure and policies), plus secretarial or project office support. In total, excluding project office support, this team comprised five people. Another example was a private company of almost 5,000 people who ran a one week pilot of information in two areas, together employing about a tenth of the workforce or about 500 people. This company had an audit team of the sponsor, two audit managers, and two subject matter experts, both of whom were management trainees and graduates in quantitative subjects. Out of the week-long period allocated to the audit the entire team spent one full day auditing , the team minus the subject matter experts spent half a day together in preparation, with the sponsor and project manager spending additional time in preparing the audit. The subject matter experts spent two or three days after the day of auditing in documenting and analysing issues to be addressed before scaling up the audit for the whole organization, and the project managers spent a day (half a day each) writing up the audit reports.

The functions that an audit team must be able to provide to the audit are:

– Project management.
– A "helpdesk" function, (i.e. assistance in using the tool.)
– Adjustment of the tool to the needs of the audit in hand.
– Preparation of the audit report.

The six attributes needed by the team as a whole are:
1. Pragmatism.
2. Personal credibility .
3. Authority over auditees.
4. A sense of purpose and urgency.
5. An understanding of organization.
6. An understanding of the value of information.

These six attributes can be put in a slightly different way. The team must have an understanding of "how to get things done" in the organization in which they are leading the audit. The team must also be capable of telling auditees to "just get on with it as best you can" or to provide coaching and assistance, and to judge which of these behaviours is appropriate and efficient. Experience of running information audits suggests that almost half of questions directed to the "helpdesk" function of the team are best answered by encouraging the requester simply to get on with it and do their best. This is for two reasons. First, the Melbourne tool is robust, and the value of the audit is little if at all impaired if a few questions about a few information assets are omitted – the really important questions are the most obvious ones, such as "Can this information cause death or injury?" and "Where is this information located?" The second reason is that the tool is very easy to learn, and once people have used it two or three times they need little assistance. Another thing that the audit team must have is an understanding of the overall strategy and purpose of the organization so that they are aware of the major sources of risk and value likely to be encountered in the course of the audit.

Let us look a little more closely at the separate roles within the audit team. Some of these may be carried out by the same individual, and we will state where a role should be carried out by someone who has no other role/s on the team.

Audit Sponsor. This role is fully described in the *Terminology* section of this chapter, above. The sponsor's role is unique and they should have no other roles in the audit.

Audit Manager. This role is fully described in the *Terminology* section of this chapter, above, and their role is also unique except in the smallest audits where the same persons may provide all the other roles except that of the sponsor.

Helpdesk. This is a vital role for the maintenance of the momentum of the audit. There must be someone available whenever a call or email comes in from one of the audit areas asking for assistance, especially at the start of the audit. The person fulfilling this role must have two attributes. First, expertise in using the tool. Secondly, an understanding of human nature so that they can say "just get on with it as best you can," which is usually most of the time, or alternatively to provide assistance and the judgement to know which of these alternatives to pick in which cases. There are no IT skills required for the helpdesk function. One of the most successful information audit helpdesk people that the authors have seen was a locum lawyer who took on the task as an additional duty while acting as an in-house solicitor-advocate. This is not a unique role and may be held by someone who is also a subject matter expert.

Subject Matter Experts. (The term is a project management term). The need for this role increases as the size of the audit increases, and the main way in which they add value to the audit process is by assisting and thereby leveraging the work done by the audit manager and the helpdesk. It is not in fact necessary that they are experts in anything except some minimal level of expertise in the information audit, but it is highly desirable that each of them has expert knowledge in one of the following areas:
- the structure and processes of the organization as a whole, or some key audit area.
- the IT systems of the organization.
- the records management function of the organization.
- the strategic aims of and risks facing the

organization.

The role of the subject matter expert is not unique and the helpdesk person may also be a subject matter expert. It is best, in any case, if the subject matter experts learn information audit helpdesk skills as soon as possible.

It must be stressed that the level of expertise referred to in the preceding paragraphs is no more than that which can readily be acquired by spending half a day undertaking information audits. The easiest way to do this is to audit the information assets that one uses in the course of one's work duties, and often one's PC will contain more than enough information assets on which to practice and, if not, one's office or workplace should.

Finalizing the audit team should not take much time. By this stage in the audit process the sponsor, if not the audit manager, should already have a shortlist of team members in mind, and most of the time required, if any, will be spent facilitating the agreement of their line managers to them taking on these responsibilities. One piece of information which is often useful in this facilitation is how much time will team members, other than the project manager and sponsor, have to devote to the proposed information audit duties? One way to answer this is to undertake a detailed project plan and try to estimate the effort required. This is not advisable, for many reasons; chiefly that the roles tend to be such that work expands to fit whatever time is allocated, and also because so many factors affect the time required and thus estimates tend to be inaccurate. Experience suggests that the most time that line managers are comfortable to allow to be taken up by any secondary duties of their staff is between half a day and one day per week. It is often best, therefore, to approach the question from this perspective and assume and state that between half a day and one day per week will be required.

9. Finalize the audit plan.

For an audit of any size there should be an audit plan. This is no more than basic project management sense and, indeed, management sense. Project management is beyond the scope of this book and we will not say much about how to produce plans. It is a good principle to use, whatever the standard project management methodology for the organization being audited – these days most organizations, both private and public sector, have their own standards for project management.

The audit plan is the output of this step in the audit process and it will be a document or set of documents that is an evolution of the project charter or mandate, which was described above in *3. Agree a mandate or charter for the audit*. In addition to the headings in the project charter, the plan should include:
- the names of the auditees.
- the list of auditees (and if there are any their designates.)
- the statement of scope.
- a` description of how the audit will run, from the point of view of the auditees, including what is expected of them and what assistance will be given to them.
- instructions for how to use the tool, and copies of the tool template.

- a timetable showing the key dates and milestones.

The key dates and milestones to include are:
- the start and finish dates for the project.
- dates for information and training sessions about the audit.
- dates for a pilot phase of the project, if there is to be one.
- when each audit area starts auditing and when it is to be complete.
- the date for completing the final report.

The plan should be made by the audit manager under the direction of the sponsor. If the previous eight steps in the audit process have been followed and if the manager is already familiar with their organization's standard project management methodology, then producing the plan will take little time.

The way to produce the plan is to follow the standard project management methodology. It is worth emphasizing, however, that the first step in the audit process, *ensure that the core audit management team understands the tool*, is vital to producing a credible plan, and that all the other preceding eight steps are also highly desirable. If an experienced project manager is tempted to skip any of them they might reflect that an experienced project manager will take very little time to complete these eight steps – in other words, they are a relatively cheap insurance policy.

There are two key question to consider in creating a plan that may not arise by simply following standard project management methodology. One is the question of whether to pilot the audit tool before embarking on the main effort of the audit. Experience suggests that this is invariably a good idea. A pilot audit is quite adequate if it is members of the audit team sitting with (or on a videoconference or telephone call with) a selection of the auditees, helping them through an audit of some information assets, along the lines that the audit team themselves will have done in step 1 - *Ensure that the core audit management team understands the tool*. Once the pilot is completed then the plan should be reviewed and, if necessary, given the results of the pilot, amended. If a pilot is to be used it must be incorporated into the plan, together with time to assess the output of the pilot and its implication, and then to review and amend the plan after the pilot.

The second question is what degree of supervision or assistance should be provided by the audit team to the auditees, and the judgement to be made here is generally a matter of degree. At one extreme the auditees can be provided with instructions and left entirely to their own devices to get on with it. At the other extreme the audit team can do all the audit work, such that the only involvement of the auditees is to point the audit team towards the assets. Experience shows that it is most unusual for either extreme to be economically wise. If the auditees are left entirely to their own devices then it is most probable that inconsistencies fatal to the worth of the audit will arise; these are inconsistencies of the meaning of various critical terms in the audit, inconsistencies in resolving the inevitable matters of detail that arise in the course of an audit, and inconsistencies in understanding what the aims of the audit imply for executing it; in short, providing no central

assistance or oversight leads to the results of
the audit being unusable or barely usable at
the corporate level. At the other extreme it
is uneconomic, except in audits of the most
minimal scope, to have no input from the
auditees and to rely solely on a specialist team
of auditors. The real question then is how to
balance the trade-off between taking up the time
of the auditees on the one hand and incurring
cost of having a larger audit team. Experience
suggests that the normal range of decisions
lies between providing a small audit team who
spend two hours training each audit area and
who thereafter provide a helpdesk and quality
assurance function; and on the other hand an
arrangement where the auditees provide an hour
or so a day of their time while the audit team
works full time in the audit area, referring to the
auditee only when they need clarification. In the
latter case outside contractors with specialist
expertise in information auditing may be used.

For the risk log of the project plan an information
audit project will usually have at least three risks
– these are that:
- The audit will lose momentum and grind to a
halt.
- The audit will attempt too much, that is, that
it will work at too low a level of granularity.
- That senior management does not see any
business benefit.

Any of several factors is sufficient, each on its
own, to crystallize the first risk, many of which
can also cause the second risk in our list above:
weak sponsorship, weak project management,
insufficient expertise with the tool on the part
of the audit manager or the team, lack of buy-
in among line managers. All of these risks will

be reduced if the sequence of activities in the audit process that are set out in this chapter are followed.

D. AUDIT KICKOFF

By this stage in the audit process the actual auditing has yet to start, but despite that most of the hard work for the audit team has been completed. From now on the work should, for the most part, be structured and routine. We have now reached the point where the audit itself starts, which is called the kickoff.

10. Brief the auditees.

The briefing to the auditees is the means by which they are formally told of the plan, the rationale for the audit, what they are expected to produce by way of results and how they are expected to do it. The value of the briefing is that it tells the people who are going to do most of the work, or at least to facilitate most of the work, exactly what to do. Without a briefing this will not happen.

The briefing is best done face to face by the sponsor and audit manager presenting to a room full of the auditees (or their designates.) This may not always be possible or cost-effective, in which case some other briefing mechanism should be used. Other possible mechanisms include video-conferencing, webinars, telephone conferencing and plain old-fashioned written instructions – in decreasing order of preference, as face to face contact tends to give the best chance of successful communication.

Before the briefing is given the project charter or possibly the full plan (or an edited version of it) and also the spreadsheet of the tool should be sent to those due to attend the briefing, and they should be asked to read these before the briefing. It is best if this communication is sent by the sponsor, although of course it may well have been drafted by the audit manager.

Also before the briefing be sure to allow sufficient time for the communications and logistics arrangements for a kickoff meeting. Getting one's own team together in a meeting room is quite a different proposition from arranging a kickoff meeting for a hundred or so staff. Large meeting rooms may need booking in advance, and getting large numbers to turn up to a meeting means at least giving them a week or a fortnight's notice in most organizations.

The format of the briefing should be whatever is that which the organization doing the audit would normally use. Experience suggests that there are usually three main components to the briefing, in the following sequence:

1.   **Introduction, scene setting and rationale.** The aim of this is to set the context for the audit, show why it matters in business terms to the organization and, above all, to motivate all involved to apply themselves to making it happen and to achieving a successful audit. The sponsor is usually the best person to deliver this section because they will usually have the greatest positional and reputational authority over the audience; the kinds of authority which matter in this part of the briefing.

2.   **Talk though the project plan.** The aim of this is to ensure that everyone involved in the project knows the plan, because that makes success more likely. This is best done by the

audit manager, as they should have the most detailed grasp of the plan of anyone, and also because this is an opportunity to impress on those in the audience that this person is the audit manager. The audit manager derives authority in this part of the briefing from expert knowledge, which in this case is knowledge of the plan. They will also be, so to speak, publicly invested with the referred authority of the sponsor.

4.   **Talk through the audit tool**. This is the main aim of the briefing, which is to ensure that the auditees learn about the tool. Experience suggests that a briefing alone is not sufficient to get the average auditee to a stage where they can audit on their own, but it is also the case that a kickoff briefing is a good thing because it creates momentum and does a significant part of the job of transferring skills to the auditees.

11. Initiate the audit.

This is the easiest step in the audit process. It is simply to tell those doing the audit, which is the audit team and the auditees, to start as per the plan. The output of this is the audit activity itself. How long it will take depends on the volume (that is number and size) of information assets to be audited and the skill and efficiency of the auditees and audit team, and also the quality of the audit plan. How it happens will have been set out in the plan, and if the plan included a pilot phase then the plan may have been revised to take account of the lessons learnt in the pilot phase. In a large audit there may be many initiations of work, because there may be many different audit areas, more than the audit team could manage at once.

12. Monitor the audit and manage by exceptions.

In this step the audit team helps the individual audit areas to complete the audit. The audit team, particularly the sponsor and the audit manager, also monitor progress, identify issues and communicate. What all this means is described in more detail below. The two main outputs are completed audits (or partially completed ones) from the audit areas and interim audit reports and other communication, formal and informal, from the project sponsor assisted by the project manager.

The best way to manage an information audit once it is in progress, once it has been initiated, is to manage by exception. The audit manager is key here. They will need to be diligent and to apply considerable effort to this management task if the audit is of any size. The audit manager must divide their attention between two equally important aspects of the audit. One aspect is the overall picture of where the audit is going, that is what are the emerging results and issues, how is the audit progressing against the overall plan and, more importantly, how is it progressing against the strategic needs of the organization and the expectations of the sponsor and audit manager? The audit manager must act swiftly to any exceptions against these, and they must communicate clearly and unambiguously to the sponsor for anything significant. The other aspects that demand the attention of the audit manager are the results or work in progress of the individual audit areas. The audit manager must review the results as they come in, although they may delegate this in a large audit. Even in a large audit, however, the

audit manager must have a system in place for
monitoring the results and identifying when,
although the auditee has not asked for help, help
ought to be sent.

Experience suggests that the following five are
some of the common issues of which the audit
manager and their team should be alert to while
managing the audit in progress:

1. Treatment of similar sets of information.
2. The level of granularity or detail at which to
    audit.
3. Getting bogged down in detail.
4. Meanings of certain audit terms – ownership,
    golden source, sharing, custodian, deprival
    value.
5. Unambiguous naming of business processes.

Treatment of similar sets of information.
The typical problem here is that in the same
audit area there exist a number different versions
of information. These different versions are
different, but very similar. For example, one is
an electronic version; the next is identical except
for it being a hard copy print-out; the next is
identical to the previous hard copy version
but includes signatures or some other minor
addition; and so on. It is often the case that a
significant body of opinion among the auditees
wants to treat all of these assets as one single
asset.

This should not be done, for one or two
reasons. If the audit is being done to satisfy the
requirement for an information audit of the
Freedom of Information Act (or if it is being done
as part of compliance with the Data Protection
Act or the Environmental Impact Regulations),

then it will render the information audit almost pointless with regard to the Act. The Act is clear that every single different version of information must be disclosed. If the audit were to count different versions as one asset, then there it is much more cumbersome to ensure the disclosure of all versions, and in practice it is much easier for individuals to arrange to circumvent the disclosure of every version identified in the asset.

Of course not all information audits are conducted for the purpose of the Freedom of Information Act. There is still a second reason for making every version of the same information a separate audit. Two of the ways that an information audit identifies and helps to achieve efficiency and effectiveness gains is by identifying unnecessary duplication of information holdings so that they can be eliminated and, secondly, by identifying areas where there is a critical risk of similar but different information sources being confused or, if the risk is not critical, there is a risk of excess cost arising from unnecessary reconciliation of similar sets of information.

Experience shows that it is almost invariably the case that audit areas will spend time arguing about how to count the number of assets where there are similar but different sets of information. It is strongly recommended, however, that any two sets of information that are not absolutely identical are counted as two sets. At least three quarters of the value of doing the audit is otherwise lost, and probably more.

The level of granularity or detail at which to audit.
Sometimes auditees and less experienced

members of the audit management team become so enamoured by the idea and process of the audit that they are tempted to take the audit down to a fine level of detail. This problem is compounded because in an audit of any size there is considerable latitude to apply judgement as to what level of granularity to go down to in the audit. As a rule of thumb, experienced information auditors say that sometimes the level of a room, in the case of paper documents, is sufficient, and usually one should not audit at below the level of a filing cabinet; although in exceptional cases one may need to audit the occasional drawer within the cabinet, cases such as very high value or mission critical information. That is, the information asset, if paper, will not be smaller than a filing cabinet and will often be an entire room of paper. This rule of thumb is of course not helpful when looking at electronic records, because of the variance in file size: for example, the same information can be 200KB if held as a data file but 2MB or more if printed out and scanned in, so size may be no guide for electronic data.

Note that just now we said "although in exceptional cases one may need to audit the occasional drawer within the cabinet, cases such as very high value or mission critical information." This is the nub of the problem. Most often it is not useful and will make the audit too slow and too expensive to audit at this level. But much of the highest value information in many organizations is – even if it is on paper rather than electronic – very small in size.

One of the weaknesses of the traditional approach to information auditing, but not the MIAMY approach, is that it ignores such realities of how organizations actually work. History is replete with illustrations of this point. In the UK the foot and mouth crisis in farming was solved largely by the information within a single file held by the Ministry of Defence on the lessons learned from the previous outbreak in the 1960s. The secrets of the atom bomb betrayed to the communists from the West by Klaus Fuchs and his fellow travellers were in a very small size. The infamous dossier that the UK government tried to claim proved that Iraq had significant quantities of so-called weapons of mass destruction (nuclear, biological and chemical weapons in plain language) in 2003 was a very large file, and it would have been a complete waste of time to audit any of it. The US Constitution, the UK's Bill of Rights and the 39 Articles of the Church of England are, or were in their time, very valuable and influential documents, but would fail the "never go below a filing cabinet" rule of thumb. More prosaically, many chief executives rely on a very small set of critical information to run their businesses.

So what? The tradition in library and records management, and many of the older schools of information auditing, is to ignore information assets that are small. The rationale for this is very understandable, but, it is clear, flawed. The problem is that considerable judgement is required to decide when to ignore small information assets, such as posters, miscellaneous files, out of date files and so on, and on the other hand how to recognize those small assets that are mission critical.

Getting bogged down in detail.
The kind of mind which enjoys information auditing seems often to be the kind of mind that

likes detail and perhaps is less interested in the big picture. Even if this theory is inaccurate, experience shows that getting bogged down in detail is a problem for up to a third of the auditees in a typical audit. Fortunately, experience also reveals that the problem is greatest in the mind of the auditees before they have much actual experience of doing the audit. That is, the thought of how to deal with detail becomes a reason for not starting the audit and a source of ever more hypothetical elaborations of reasons not to start and why the audit might not work. In one sense it could be said that it would be ideal if such people could be forced at gunpoint to get a move on, because experience further reveals that even one or two hours and no more overcomes this problem, but that would probably be counterproductive in practice, for all sorts of reasons. However, the idea illustrates the challenge for the helpdesk function and their task, which is to coax those auditees who are reluctant to get stuck in to make a start and apply their full effort to the audit.

Meanings of certain audit terms

There are a number of terms used in the information audit which need to be defined tightly if the audit is to be consistent across the organization, but which can only be sufficiently tightly defined through practical experience in the organization being audited. This is because some of the meanings will vary from case to case. Sometimes, similarly, a word has a precise definition but it is not used that way or not used at all in the organization doing the audit, but the word catches the imagination of the auditees who decide to impart their own meaning to it – there is nothing wrong with this at all, provided all auditees agree to it having the same meaning. Some of the words which may occasion this problem include: "ownership", "golden source", "sharing", "custodian", "deprival value".

To take just one of these as an example, consider the term "golden source[6]." This is a technical term used by those who have applied total quality management techniques (TQM) such as six-sigma to information and IT management. It means that a source of information has been designated as the sole source of such information to be used for anything, so whenever that information is required, only the golden source is used. This reduces the effort and risk which arises from reconciliations and uncertainty when there are several possible sources of the same information. Strictly speaking, the term only applies where the organization has formally adopted TQM thinking and has designated certain sources of information as golden sources. If the attribute for "golden source" is left in the audit template to be used by an organization that has not adopted such thinking, what happens is that many auditees like the idea so much that they start to apply it themselves, usually to mean that they would like such and such a source of information to be designated a golden source. While this is positive in that it shows and indeed may even encourage buy-in to the audit, there are risks in it. First, should the organization adopt TQM in information management at a later date, the pre-existing (and incorrect) designations may cause risk. And the second risk is that if the term is to be used to bring about the results that such enthusiastic early adopters hope, and which has occasioned their enthusiasm, it is a designation over which there must be some central control: people cannot

designate golden sources without reference to
the overall information architecture – this is the
whole point of a golden source, if one thinks
about it. To recall the point that we are using this
example to illustrate, the job of the audit team
in this example is to decide whether to keep the
term "golden source" in the audit, and if so then
if it is not a TQM organization, to ensure that
auditees use it in a consistent way. (Whether
consistently right or wrong from a theoretical
perspective is not important.)

It is not likely to help most readers to run
through the entire list of such possible cases
and describe them here, nor is it efficient. The
next chapter gives an adequate definition of all
terms used in the audit, except for those defined
in this chapter. The greatest need under this
heading is for the audit team to be aware of the
problem and to identify and resolve it as it arises,
whatever is the particular term at issue.

Unambiguous naming of business processes.
Information exists to support business processes,
such as making decisions. A particular
information asset will be associated with certain
business processes and not with others. A large
part of the task of running an organization well
is optimizing processes and identifying sources
of risk in those processes. In either case it is
valuable to know which information asset is
associated with which decision.

Many corporate and government scandals boil
down to nothing more than mistakes, sometimes
felt by some to be deliberate or close to being
deliberate, in associating the wrong information
asset with a decision.

The information about the existence of so-called weapons of mass destruction was a vital input to the UK government's decision to join the US in waging war in Iraq in 2003. (In contrast, the information that the UK has a treaty obligation to assist the US because the US had been attacked was not connected to the decision, although it may have seemed to some to have been a more credible connexion to make).

The oil giant, Shell, stepped in shortly after the Gulf War to show that the public sector has no monopoly on this confusion over which information assets connect to which processes. The chairman of Shell had to resign after Shell fell under heavy criticism for over-booking oil reserves, that is asserting that it had rights to rather more oil in the ground than its shareholders and financial markets regulators felt was justified. Shell's problem can be seen as connecting the wrong information assets – because there were more conservative estimates of oil reserves in existence – to its strategic forecasting and investor relations processes. The ex-chairman, however, remained fully connected to his ample final bonus.

Whatever the mistakes of the UK government and of Shell, if indeed they were mistakes, correcting such mistakes will be hard if business processes are not clearly identified. At the time of writing it is not the case that most organizations have a system for identifying their business processes, although some, especially those operating in very high risk areas such as aircraft operations or nuclear power, have moved a long way in the right direction.

The point is that in order to identify what

information is flowing into which business process, identifying the information asset is only half the problem. Identifying the business process is the other half of the problem. This problem does not really exist within the audit areas but is much more likely to between them, especially if different audit areas call the same process by different names or are not aware of the business processes in which their information is used in other audit areas. Until organizations improve their knowledge over what processes they have, there is nothing that can be done in this area as far as the audit is concerned except to ensure that the team has an understanding of how the organization works in terms of processes. In practice this means that at least one of the subject matter experts should have such knowledge.

13. *Identify, exploit and communicate quick wins.*

A quick win means a demonstrable business benefit that comes early in the project. "Early" means six weeks in the private sector and three months in the public sector. OK – we exaggerate, and there are no hard and fast rules about timescales, and it is unfair to imply that the private sector has such a different sense of urgency when many of the private sector train companies and many of the airlines that the authors have travelled with would make a stopped clock look speedy. But it makes the point, which is that the information audit must produce tangible, positive results well within the immediate time horizon of the organization within which it is being conducted. It must get results fast. It is largely up to the audit manager to make this happen, and the audit sponsor should ensure that they do and assist, especially in identifying likely candidates for quick wins.

It may be helpful to give some examples of quick
wins that information audits have delivered.
Two are given in Table 3.7.

Table 3.7 – Examples of quick wins from information audits

Quick win 1 – Private sector engineering company

The first day of an information audit produced data which indicated that potential
cost reductions of between £300,000 and £600,000 per year were probable, simply by
eliminating duplicate holdings of paper records, and that further cost savings were
likely if modest investments were to be made in storing the information contained in
the remaining records electronically instead of printing it out of electronic systems
and storing it as paper. A further week of more detailed business analysis supported
this initial finding. The information audit also gained the support and approval of
the corporate knowledge management team very quickly, because they saw in it a
means to obtain vital information about the actual flows and usages of information in
parts of the organization where they did not have visibility.

Quick win 2 – Public sector

This local authority piloted an information audit in its legal service and then initiated
an information audit across all functions. Quick wins included: one function
discarded one third of its holdings of paper files as part of its preparations for the
audit, freeing up space and reducing the sense of stress on staff. Another function
identified three databases performing the same function, but with inconsistent data
sets and necessitating the use of temporary staff. The area was rationalized to one
system, one set of data, and the temporary staff were no longer needed. Significant
cost savings and a reduction in operational risk resulted. The audit assisted in
prioritizing and re-energizing the programme of work to improve the quality of staff
records, which were a major source of risk.

It is absolutely no use identifying quick wins if they are not communicated up the chain and laterally to those who should know about them. Communication is a vital activity for the audit manager and the audit sponsor during this stage of the audit process. How to communicate within organizations is outside the scope of this manual, although it should be noted that both informal and formal reporting should be used as part of the overall communications plan. It should also be noted that like any other project, an information audit project should identify complementary initiatives and build links into them so that all complementary projects, including the information audit, benefit from sharing and jointly increasing the momentum and buy-in to the projects.

An example of a detailed interim audit report is given at Table 3.8, to show the kinds of message that has been thought useful and valuable by other organizations who have carried out an information audit. This example is taken from the report on the pilot stage of an audit, but the reader will easily be able to adapt it for a final report.

It is not unusual for the audit reports at the interim or pilot stages to be lengthier than the final reports (except for the annex containing the full audit results) because the interim reports are serving also to communicate new ideas, obtain buy-in, make various businesses cases and do other things that tend to be needed in the early stages rather than the later stages of the audit. The example in Table 3.8 contains much of such additional material; the knowledge management project referred to in the audit report is an example of what we meant, above,

82

by a complementary project.

The single thing that makes the most difference in this step is having a sponsor or some member of the audit team who has a nose for credible quick wins in the organization.

14. Close the audit.

The first thing to do in closing the audit is to hand over the main output of the audit, that is the audit spreadsheet or database or web-database itself, to the person designated by the organization to own or maintain the audit data. This person may be called the Information Officer. Absent an Information Officer other functions who sometimes own the audit data are the company secretary, the head of legal services, the finance director, the head of knowledge management, or the head of internal audit.

The second thing to do once the audit is complete is to formally close the audit. At the very least this means that the audit manager should give a verbal report to the sponsor (this is not the audit report described below in the next paragraph) and that the sponsor should record their decision that the audit is completed and let the audit team and the auditees know. The procedure for closing projects in particular organizations will usually include other project closedown activities, and the audit is a project and should follow whatever are the normal project management processes.

Thirdly, there will usually be made some sort of final audit report, including a list of recommendations. The nature and purpose of audit reports was described in the last section and an example was given there in Table 3.8. The final audit report is simply an updated version of the interim report, written from the perspective of the end of the audit.

SUMMARY

We have seen that there are fourteen distinct steps in conducting an information audit, although for convenience these can be grouped into five overall tasks, of which tasks 2-5 are the main ones.

- A. Prologue – familiarization.
- B. Project administration.
- C. Audit administration.
- D. Audit kickoff.
- E. Completion of the audit.

Figure 3.1 summarizes the audit process.

The audit is the responsibility of the audit sponsor and their audit team, with day-to-day audit management led by the audit manager who reports to the audit sponsor. The audit team works closely with the auditees, who are managers (or the managers' designates) of the audit areas. Up to the point of Task D, the audit kickoff, it is the audit manager and the audit team who have the most work, then from the moment of kickoff the balance of work spreads evenly between the audit team and the auditees. It is up to the audit manager to maintain momentum among the auditees after kickoff. Another key responsibility after kickoff of the audit manager is to communicate progress and findings to the rest of the organization via the sponsor. At all times the sponsor and audit team,

84

and everyone involved, must identify, seize and communicate business benefits, particularly quick wins.

Good luck!

Because the methodology was first documented systematically in Melbourne, although it was designed for use by and with input from UK organizations.

Aldersgate Partners LLP, London, internal research project 2004, private correspondence.

In the same way that in the United Kingdom, Canada, Australia and New Zealand, and many other countries, Acts of Parliament are made in the name of the Sovereign. (See for example the various Official Information Acts, Freedom of Information Acts and such like.)

We have just stated that the project charter will include the statement of purpose. This is true, in that it should. Note that the example that we reproduce here of a project charter is not from either of the organizations from which the statements of purpose were quoted in the preceding text.

Aldersgate Partners LLP interviews with a number of professional archivists and records managers 2003-2004 and Aldersgate's own experience of conducting information audits, 2004.

We are grateful to Roy Varughese of Deutsche Bank for drawing our attention to this idea some time ago.

Fig. 3.1
Overview of the Melbourne Information Audit Methodology

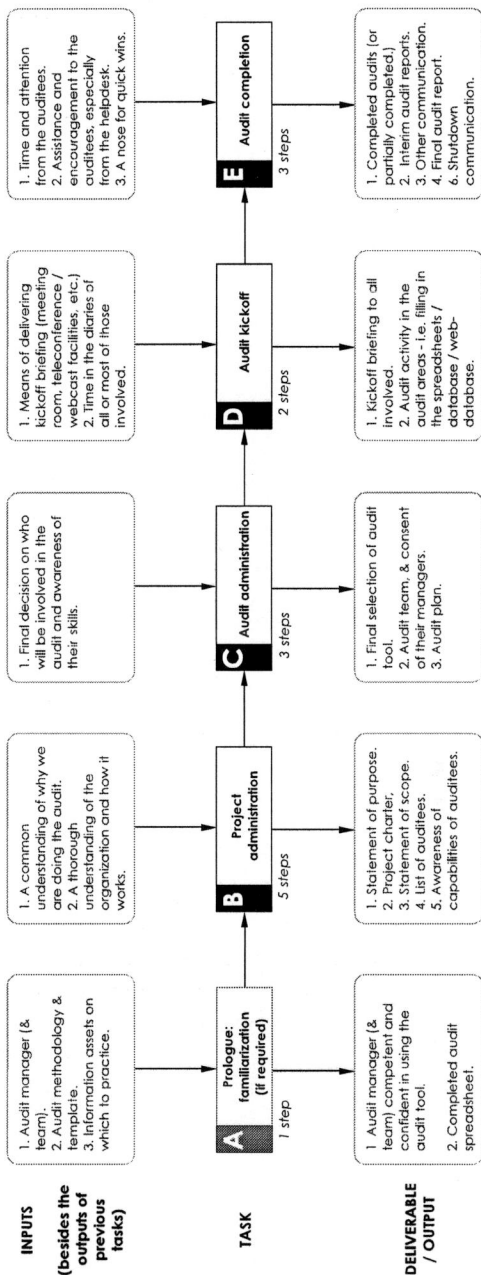

INPUTS (besides the outputs of previous tasks)	1. Audit manager (& team). 2. Audit methodology & template. 3. Information assets on which to practice.	1. A common understanding of why we are doing the audit. 2. A thorough understanding of the organization and how it works.	1. Final decision on who will be involved in the audit and awareness of their skills.	1. Means of delivering kickoff briefing (meeting room, teleconference / webcast facilities, etc.) 2. Time in the diaries of all or most of those involved.	1. Time and attention from the auditees. 2. Assistance and encouragement to the auditees, especially from the helpdesk. 3. A nose for quick wins.
TASK	**A** Prologue: familiarization (if required) 1 step	**B** Project administration 5 steps	**C** Audit administration 3 steps	**D** Audit kickoff 2 steps	**E** Audit completion 3 steps
DELIVERABLE / OUTPUT	1. Audit manager (& team) competent and confident in using the audit tool. 2. Completed audit spreadsheet.	1. Statement of purpose. 2. Project charter. 3. Statement of scope. 4. List of auditees. 5. Awareness of capabilities of auditees.	1. Final selection of audit tool. 2. Audit team, & consent of their managers. 3. Audit plan.	1. Kickoff briefing to all involved. 2. Audit activity in the audit areas - i.e. filling in the spreadsheets / database / web-database.	1. Completed audits (or partially completed.) 2. Interim audit reports. 3. Other communication. 4. Final audit report. 5. Shutdown communication.

Chapter 4

THE AUDIT TEMPLATE IN DETAIL

In this chapter we run through many of the attribute used in the Melbourne information audit (in the database or spreadsheet implementation of it these will be the field or column headings.) We explain individual attributes, show why they are used and give model answers. This chapter is in effect the manual for using the Melbourne audit tool.

OPERATIONAL FEATURES

LOCATION

What is this attribute?

This attribute simply states where the information asset is. If the asset is paper then state which room it is in; if the information asset is in electronic form and is held on a network, then state from which PCs or terminals it can be accessed; if the information is in electronic form but is on a CD or magnetic tape or some other medium than network storage, then state which room it is in, just as for paper.

If there is one, then also include in your answer to this question the name of the file series.

Why does this attribute matter? What is the business case?

The organization needs to know where its assets are. Knowing that information exists is vital, but just as vital is knowing where it is. Usually, the person who uses the information will know where it is, but there may be others in the organization for whom knowing would be very valuable and who would not usually know; common examples of such people are those responsible for Freedom of Information, Data Protection, corporate governance and cross-cutting policy.

How should the question be answered?

Simply state where the information is. If your organization has room numbers or some similar scheme such as mail points, state this number. If your organization has more than one building or location, state the town or building . Ideally the answer should be at the level of a room. It is usually excessive detail to give any location within a room, unless the room is very large.

Tips for answering this question usefully

A good answer is one that will enable someone unfamiliar with the asset to find it during a normal working day. Getting to the right room and asking someone else in that room the exact location of the asset is acceptable.

When not to use this attribute

There are no occasions on which this attribute should not be completed.

Frequently asked questions

What if we don't have room numbers?
Then the trade-off to be decided is whether to incur the administrative and bureaucratic cost of applying a room numbering scheme, or whether to have some workaround that is less costly. Usually in a large organization there will be a room numbering scheme owned by the facilities managers or building engineers, even if it is not widely known. In a small organization it is quite possible to keep an audit up-to-date without a room numbering scheme.

If you decide to use an existing but little known room-numbering scheme, then try to sell other, non-audit benefits of the scheme. There are usually health and safety benefits (e.g. reporting the exact location of an incident) and disaster recovery benefits.

Model answer

A. The filing room, 1st floor, City Hall.

90

NARRATIVE DESCRIPTION OF THE INFORMATION ASSET

What is this attribute?

This is simply a narrative description of what the asset is.

Why does this attribute matter? What is the business case?

If the title or name of the asset is not completely self-explanatory, then a short narrative description should be used to make clear exactly what the asset is. "Chief executive's personal files" is a perfectly clear title, but it is not clear to anyone unfamiliar with the files what kinds of information they contain.

How should the question be answered?

Write a short general description of the information. Between one sentence and one paragraph is sufficient.

Tips for answering this question usefully

Think of what narrative description would be most useful for someone who is familiar with the organization but not with the part of the organization within which this particular information is held.

When not to use this attribute

There are very few occasions on which this attribute should not be completed.

Frequently asked questions

Isn't this unnecessary when the name of the information asset makes it obvious what the information is about?

Possibly, but what is obvious to someone who

works with this information every day may not be obvious to someone who does not.

Model answer

A.   Files on all matters dealt with by the Chief Executive personally, including a file for each directorate, a complaints file, and files for each of the major organizations with whom the Chief Executive deals.

KEYWORDS

What is this attribute?

This attribute is a list of keywords from the information asset. A keyword is a word that is found frequently in the asset and in some way bears a significant relationship to the information asset.

Why does this attribute matter? What is the business case?

Keywords are used to search for information assets. Having a good set of keywords for an information asset increases the chances of finding the asset when it is needed. For example, suppose that there is an information asset that is all correspondence between the organization and the regulator called the Financial Services Authority, and that this asset is called "Financial Services Authority Correspondence." A search for "Financial Services Authority " or "correspondence" will lead to this asset, but a search for "FSA," "regulatory correspondence" or "FSA emails" will not. Adding these terms as keywords will ensure that searches will lead to this asset.

How should the question be answered?

Enter into this field all keywords associated with the information asset. In practice it is unlikely that too many keywords can be recorded for each asset; as a rule the more keywords the better.

Tips for answering this question usefully

Use any word, abbreviation or combination thereof that is likely to be used by people when they need to identify this information asset. If the name of the asset is specific, use keywords that are the generic descriptors of the specific name, and vice versa. The main thing is to think of the keywords that other people are likely to use when they want to retrieve this information.

When not to use this attribute

There are very few occasions on which this attribute should not be completed.

Frequently asked questions

How should keywords be chosen?

As a general rule, keyword searches are more effective the more keywords there are to search, and entering more keywords does little harm to the efficiency or effectiveness of searches. Therefore, enter as many keywords as you can think of. Make full use of any standard industry terminology, and think what keywords might be used by people from other parts of the organization and other disciplines.

Model answer

A.   Chief Executive, Chief Executive's personal files, management files, audit reports, complaints from the public, performance, best value, day book, investigations, governance, correspondence, headquarters.

WHO OWNS THIS INFORMATION ASSET?

What is this attribute?

This attribute states who owns the information asset. Ownership in this sense means the person (or the appointment) within the organization who has the greatest power to order the creation, amendment or destruction of the information asset. In practice organizations each tend to have their own, often implicit, definitions of what ownership of information or databases means, and it is that definition which should be used for the purposes of this attribute; it is unwise to create a new definition. (We should also point out that the term "ownership" here is not related to the legal or copyright ownership of the information asset).

Note that this attribute is one of two very similar attributes in the audit. The other comes later in the series of questions and is "Who owns this information asset? (Post and telephone extension)." This first attribute is asking about the category of owner, whereas the second question is asking who is the particular, specific owner.

Why does this attribute matter? What is the business case?

Assets that have no owner tend to be poorly looked after. Assets that are disputed by two would-be owners can be a source of friction, risk and inefficiency in the organization. The owner of an asset is the ultimate decision maker on investing in the asset, maintaining it and deciding who else may use and modify it. There can really be only one owner of an asset; where an asset is jointly owned, that is owned by two or more people or functions, it is in effect owned by a single partnership comprised of all these owners. To see what this claim means consider what happens in practice if a database, say, is jointly owned by the finance function and also the human resources function, compared to what happens when just one function, say, finance, owns a database. When the database is jointly owned and one of the joint owners wants to make some change, for example to delete a field in all records in the database, that owner will check with the other owner before taking any action, and may indeed modify its plans for taking action depending on the views of the other owner. Whereas if the database has only a single owner, then the owner alone decides whether to make the change. (There may of course be users of the database or whatever information asset it is, and if the owner has any interest in looking after the users then they would be well advised to consult the users before making changes. The vital difference between the concept of ownership and usership is that it is the owner who has the power to decide what changes should be made. This, incidentally, is the fundamental reason why it is so difficult to eliminate databases in organizations).

Put another way, ownership matters because it is the asset's owner who is best able to ensure that the asset is used as efficiently as possible.

How should the question be answered?

This question has six possible answers:

A - audit area;
B - the same organization;
C - a supplier

D - some other party;

E - it is in the public domain.

The term "audit area" refers to the part of the organization within which the audit is being conducted. In an investment bank this is typically a trading desk or a corporate finance team or, in the support functions, a group or team. In a local authority this is typically a function, and in a central government department it is normally a desk or an office. In general, it is usually the lowest level administrative or functional unit of an organization, typically comprising between four and thirty people. Answer "A," then, means that the information is owned by the audit area or by some individual or sub-group within the audit area.

"B" means that the owner is not the audit area but is still the same organization – that is the same public authority or the same firm.

"C" means that the information asset is owned by a supplier to the organization.

"D" means that the information has an owner, but not "A," "B" or "C".

It is possible that information does not have an owner in the sense that it is in the public domain, "E".

(If the owner is unknown then leave this field blank.)

Tips for answering this question usefully

If there are two versions because there are two owners, then there are in fact two information assets and each should be given a separate line in the audit. The general rule is that different versions of an information asset are really two different assets. One of the aims of the information audit is to reduce excess holdings of information assets and to reduce the effort necessary to reconcile between similar assets, and for these reasons different versions of an asset should be classified as two different assets, or else there will be no visibility of the excess. This general rule is no more than common sense, and the same principle guides us in the way that among human beings we treat identical twins – who are different versions of the same genetic assets – as two different people, each with their own set of obligations and their own creative, legal and economic potential.

When not to use this attribute

This attribute should always be completed. The only exception is when the owner is not known, in which case leave this field blank.

Frequently asked questions

What is an owner? Can there be several owners?

See above, "What is this attribute?" for the general answer to who is an owner. Sometimes the real question arises because several different parts of an organization want ownership of an information asset. Shared ownership of information assets is possible, but in our experience this solution to the problem is successful as rarely as is the sharing of senior management positions, that is to say infrequent at best – and for the same reasons. It is nearly always better to assign ownership of an information asset to one person or function only and to have service level agreements or some other formal protocol to address the competing demand for ownership.

Note that there is another question later in the audit template which asks for the name or function of the owner. In the case where two different audit areas do share ownership of a single information asset, the details of the joint owner should be recorded in the other field, i.e. "Who owns this information asset? (Post and telephone extension)", and this field should be completed as "B" – the same organization.

Model answer

A.   Chief Executive.

WITH WHAT OTHER INFORMATION ASSETS IS THIS ASSET CLOSELY ASSOCIATED? HOW?

What is this attribute?

This attribute lists other information assets with which this asset is closely associated. Close association means either closely associated content or process. In other words, respectively, this asset comprises information that is similar to another asset's, or that this information asset is used in (or created by) the same business process as other information assets.

Why does this attribute matter? What is the business case?

There are two reasons why it may be useful to know what information assets are closely associated with each other. First, there may be synergistic opportunities, that is opportunities to reduce and rationalize a number of different assets. This is particularly so as the audit methodology requires similar but different assets to be classified as separate assets – if we do this we should retain some means of knowing that they are similar. The second reason is that when using the information audit to help understand or think about processes, it may be useful to know what other assets there are in adjacent parts of the process. Of course if we already have a complete and up-to-date process map this will not be necessary, but that happy scenario is rarely the actual case, and so there can be great benefit to being able to obtain this knowledge from the information audit.

How should the question be answered?

List the other information assets with which this one is associated. Use the names of the assets as they appear in their own entries in the audit.

Tips for answering this question usefully

Where more than one naming convention is used, enter all the names for each asset.

When not to use this attribute

There is no need to force an association, that is to try to think one up where there is no obvious association with another asset.

Model answers

A.   It is a collation of three other information assets, (1) the summary pages of the quarterly audit reports, (2) the Chief Executive's personal quarterly agenda, and (3) the risk register with a narrative added.

B.   It is a hardcopy of the environmental disposal certificate, with an officer's signature added.

C.   It is an edited and downgraded version of the internal disciplinary enquiries, but downgraded and redacted from a protective marking of CONFIDENTIAL to UNCLASSIFIED.

STRUCTURE

What is this attribute?

This attribute describes the level of structure in the information asset. An artist's colony tends to be an unstructured organization, whereas an infantry battalion poised for war is a highly structured organization. Medium sized law firms tend to be somewhere in between. We probably wouldn't want to offer very much for pictures painted by the infantry soldiers, and nor would we want the artist to organize our defence if facing attack by an enemy army. And so it is with information; the structure should suit the purpose. We want our bank statements to be highly structured; they would be no good if the entries were all over the page, *a la* Kandinsky: but we expect a little more latitude in papers analysing new and unknown problems.

This attribute is about the degree of structure that there is in an information asset.

Why does this attribute matter? What is the business case?

Structured information is cheaper to manage once created and has less risk inhering in than unstructured information, but the processes for creating structured information can have high set-up costs. The paradigm example of structured information is a database. Each entry in the database, that is each record, costs little to manage, but the database itself may have cost much to design and set-up.

Unstructured information is often very low cost to produce, the paradigm case being a handwritten note. However, searching within a room full of handwritten notes for one particular

nugget of information is very costly, and there is
no alternative to having a person reading each
note line by line. Even if this is done offshore it is
still an expensive process.

The structure of information is fundamental
to its economic properties, and this is why we
record this attribute.

How should the question be answered?

For the purposes of the information audit we
have three possible answers.

"S" - Structured
"T" - Semi-structured
"U" - Unstructured

Tips for answering this question usefully

It is possible to waste much time debating or
pondering what semi-structured information
is. It is best if your organization formulates its
own definitions of structured, semi-structured
and unstructured information. The people who
should be involved in creating such definitions
are the legal department, the IT department, the
finance department, the policy or performance
department and, if there is one, the information
management department.

If there is no definition, the fastest way to
proceed is to ignore the term "semi-structured"
and to define structured information as any
information that is either held in a database or
could be entered without modification in any
way into a database.

In any case, if in doubt, an information asset should be categorized as unstructured.

When not to use this attribute

This attribute should always be used.

Frequently asked questions

Can paper-based information be structured?

Yes. A card-index is an example. A set of completed templates – such as a set of end of term reports for a class of schoolgirls – is another example.

IN WHAT FORMAT IS THE INFORMATION?

What is this attribute?

Just as colours do not exist independently of some object in which they inhere, there is no information but that it is recorded on some medium, for example paper or magnetic tape or CD-ROM. Information will be managed in potentially quite different ways according to what type of media it is recorded. Even if one manages to fit the A4 file of paper into the disk drive of the PC, nothing useful will result. More prosaically, if we want 100 copies of some piece of information in a form which people can read (without the aid of a PC) then if the original is in A4 paper format we will need a photocopier to make the 100 copies, but if it is in a word-processor format on a CD-ROM then we will need a PC and a printer.

Why does this attribute matter? What is the business case?

The point is that the information audit can help the organization to exploit its information holdings to the fullest possible extent, but a critical factor in doing this is that we must know the format in which each piece of information is held.

How should the question be answered?

The answer to this audit question has a primary answer, "X", which in some cases may be followed by a descriptor "- YYYY" so that a full answer is in the form "X - YYYY…Y" – as follows:

"P" - Paper, with format descriptor, e.g. P - A0, P - A4, P - 8vo, etc.

"E" - Electronic, held in an IT system's internal memory (no descriptor).
"D" - Disc, with format descriptor, e.g. D - DVD, D - 8", D - CD-ROM etc.
"T" - magnetic tape, stating format descriptor e.g. T - 0.75", T - VHS, etc.
"C" - punched card (no descriptor)
"X" - animal skin or parchment (no descriptor)
"O" - other (no descriptor)

Tips for answering this question usefully

Be as specific with the descriptors as possible; they need not be confined to the list above.

When not to use this attribute

This attribute should always be completed.

Frequently asked questions

If there are two formats in which we hold the information asset, e.g. paper and electronic, is that one asset or two?

Two. Even if the information is identical in both formats, the audit should state that there are two assets by recording each asset as a separate entry. This is because one of the aims of the information audit is to enable redundant holdings of information to be eliminated, and first of all, redundant information is easiest to identify if different formats of the same information are recorded as separate assets, and secondly, when one of the formats is discarded it is easier and less work to delete an entire asset then to go through an entry and modify it.

Model answers

A.   T - VHS
B.   P - A4

IF PAPER, WHAT FACTORS WOULD AFFECT REPLACING IT WITH AN ELECTRONIC VERSION?

What is this attribute?

This attribute only applies if the asset is held in a paper format – which the previous audit question established.

Why does this attribute matter? What is the business case?

Information held in paper format costs more to store and manage and is harder to search and transmit than the same information held in an electronic format.

How should the question be answered?

List the factors that would affect converting this paper information asset into an electronic format. See "Model Answers" below for examples. N.B. factors can be positive – that is in favour of converting to electronic format – as well as negative or against conversion.

Tips for answering this question usefully

Find the main users of the information and get them to think through whether or not it would be useful to them if the information was in electronic instead of paper form. Often they will already have thought this through. Consider the practicalities, especially whether merely scanning will result in useful information or whether some sort of OCR conversion will also be required. If the paper to be scanned is larger than A4, what size is it and are suitable scanners available? Architectural and engineering plans, for example, are often larger than A4 and even A3.

When not to use this attribute

If the asset is not in paper form, or if it is paper if it is retained for a very short time only, say one day or less.

Model answers

A.   Already have electronic copies of half of it, the outgoing material. Scanning in the incoming material would be a good idea.

B.   1 – *Time.* We don't have time to scan the documents; 200 days required.
2 – *Cost.* We don't have sheet-fed bulk scanners; they are £4000 to buy or £1900 to hire for 250 days. An alternative is a service, but cost per page is 5p, x 200,000 sheets = £10,000.
3 – *Skill.* Apart from managerial staff, none of our staff know how to use scanners and software.
4 – *Optical Character Recognition* (OCR). Scanning alone will not improve the utility of this information; indeed we may be worse off if we disposed of this paper asset and replaced it with scans of images (i.e. no OCR). So we would also need to OCR this material if we scanned it, which would add to the costs, though not the time, shown above.

C.   Scanning this information and disposing of the paper would pay for itself within one year. We only need the cover page of each box file because it references the same information held in a government agency. We rarely need the information, and when we do it is always referred to by date. Scanning the 6,000 cover pages and filing them will cost £6,000, but the cost of the space occupied by the 6,000 box files is about the same. We are short of space and could use the space thus released to house Project Diamond instead of renting temporary space.

GOLDEN SOURCE

A golden source of information is a source of some particular piece of information that is designated as the most reliable and accurate source. By way of examples, rumour is not a golden source of any piece of information; by contrast if the information is, say, the time, then the speaking clock or the atomic clock at the Royal Observatory could be potential golden sources of their respective pieces of information. But we say *potentially* in both these examples because to be a golden source the source of information must not only be the most accurate source, it must be designated as such by the organization.

Take the example of personnel information, say, the dates of birth of staff. This information – that is these dates of birth – will be required by various different groups within one organization: by human resources staff to complete staff records, by line managers, by actuaries to calculate pensions, by IT staff to verify identity and passwords, and so on. This means that the same information will exist in many different forms. Suppose that an error creeps into a record of somebody's date of birth; suppose that the pensions data is mis-keyed. Later on the board orders a review of ageism in the organization and new records are set up for this purpose, including dates of birth. These records take the dates of birth from existing pension records, and the error is propagated. Later, someone in HR notices that the pensions record for this employee shows a different date of birth than the record of hiring. To track down which is

wrong, HR looks at a third version, but not
knowing that it is a copy of the incorrect data,
selects for this purpose the equality records.
In this example, whenever there is a need to
replicate some existing piece of information
and there are several possible existing sources
of the information, there is no central control
on which of the several possible sources are
used to supply that information. (This kind
of laxity over information management is
widespread. Whatever its motives in invading
Iraq, the UK government was not aware that
its "dodgy dossier" on Iraq contained old
information plagiarized from an academic thesis
on Internet at the time it published its dossier).
A consequence of this uncontrolled sourcing of
information is that errors are propagated and
then expensive reconciliation and data cleansing
processes have to be used.

The alternative is to designate one particular
source of one type of information as the golden
source. Then when that information is needed it
is the golden source and only the golden source
that is used. No "copies of copies" are allowed.

Why does this attribute matter? What is the business case?

Adopting a golden source approach to
information management means that the
golden source must be kept clean and its quality
assured, but the cost of doing this once with just
the golden source is far less than the costs and
risks of the alternative.

How should the question be answered?

Yes or No.

Tips for answering this question usefully

If in doubt, then "No" is the correct answer.

When not to use this attribute

The golden source approach to information management means something only if it is adopted across the whole organization, which means that it must be mandated by senior management. If your organization has not adopted the golden source model, then do not use this attribute.

WITH WHAT BUSINESS PROCESS IS THE INFORMATION ASSOCIATED?

What is this attribute?

This attribute applies particular information assets to particular business processes.

Why does this attribute matter? What is the business case?

All information exists to support some business process, or as the final output of a business process. Management information, for example, exists to support decision making, or it is the result of having made a decision. Recently managers have come to see the value of taking a process view of their organizations, and every process in an organization is associated with certain information assets. The performance of those processes, their efficiency and effectiveness and also the risk of their outputs, is critically dependent on the quality of the information assets used as inputs or used to control the processes. In short, "garbage in, garbage out." One of the key steps in improving business processes is to ensure that information used in those processes is of sufficient quality, and to do this the organization needs to know what information assets are associated with each process.

How should the question be answered?

Name each business process for which this asset is either an input or an output. ("Input" and "output" here include controlling information, which in some business process mapping methodologies (for example IDEF0) categorize separately).

Tips for answering this question usefully

> If there is an official list of names of business processes or a numbering scheme, use that and nothing else in answering the question. If there is no such official list, then give a short description of the business process that will mean something to anyone else whose work touches that process.

When not to use this attribute

> If your organization has no interest in process thinking.

Model answers

> A.   (Assume that the information asset in question is "Annual employee performance review"). Staff bonus annual calculations; promotions process; 360 degree feedback process; disciplinary process.

> B.   (Assume that the information in question is timesheets for in-house lawyers).
> 1 – Cost allocation
> 2 – Capacity forecasting
> 3 – Management reporting in Legal Services

> C.   (Assume that the information is recordings of readings from a monitor to be used for chemical analysis of weekly samples of effluent discharged into a river).
> > Process # 2017.B   Internal monitoring of effluent
> > Process # 3001.A   Environment Agency reporting
> > Process # 5328.3   Analysis of effluent
> readings

HOW IS IT ASSOCIATED?

What is this attribute?

>This attribute derives from the preceding one and is asking how the information is associated with those business processes with which it is associated.

Why does this attribute matter? What is the business case?

>This information can add value to process optimization or process re-engineering projects by providing such projects with critical information and avoiding the need to spend effort within such projects on obtaining this information. It costs little to obtain such information during an information audit compared to obtaining it specially during a process optimization or process re-engineering project.

>This information may also be valuable if an organization is evaluating or monitoring the risks in its processes, because a significant source of risk is the quality of information associated with those processes.

How should the question be answered?

>I - Inputs
>O - Outputs
>C - Constraints
>M - Control mechanisms
>X - Unknown

Tips for answering this question usefully

>If in doubt enter "X".

If the previous attribute in the audit is not used, then this attribute is superfluous.

Frequently asked questions

What is IDEF0?
IDEF0 or IDEF is one of the standard models for mapping business processes.

Model answers

These three examples are continuations of and make the same assumptions as the examples given for the previous attribute.

A.   Input.

B.   1 – The entire input
2 – The main input
3 – A minor input

C.   (Assume that the information is chemical analysis recordings of weekly samples of effluent discharged into a river).

Process # 2017.B	Input
Process # 3001.A	Input
Process # 5328.3	Output

116

IS THERE A DESCRIPTION OR MAP OF THE PROCESS?

What is this attribute?

It is simply a statement of whether there exists a map of the business process; the process has been the subject of the previous two attributes.

Why does this attribute matter? What is the business case?

Creating process maps is a costly affair, but the resulting maps are useful for many management purposes. If a map exists they should be available to any manager who needs them, but often in organizations that have invested in creating process maps they are not available and are often not known about beyond the part of the business that created them.

How should the question be answered?

Answer "Yes" or "No"; if "Yes", add the file name of the map and where it is located.

Model answer

Finance department files, M5 Plans, <<040115 Finance BPR Maps 1.13.201>>.

WHAT IS THE SOURCE OF THE INFORMATION? FROM WHERE DO YOU GET IT?

What is this attribute?

This attribute is a narrative description of where the information comes from. In a previous attribute we have recorded where the information is held, or to say it another way, where is it stored, but in this attribute we say where the asset comes from, or to put it another way, where was it stored before where it is stored now?

Why does this attribute matter? What is the business case?

If the same information is being stored in many places in the organization there is probably an opportunity to rationalize matters and have one copy of the information but make it accessible to all those who need it. There is especially likely to be significant benefits from doing this if the asset is already in electronic form.

If an asset is being procured from outside the organization, this attribute (together with the "Owner" attribute) will help to identify opportunities to economize in procurement if more than one copy of the same information is being procured by different parts of the organization.

How should the question be answered?

List the sources of the information.

Tips for answering this question usefully

Be specific. Name the source. Don't enter "A supplier," but rather "Bleuters News Systems," or "The financial controller of the Maestro

25

118

Division" for example. If the information asset is created from scratch by the audit area, then say so; and if the information is created from other assets within the audit area, again say so here.

When not to use this attribute

This attribute should always be used.

Frequently asked questions

How do I know where we get the information from?

Someone will know where each information asset comes from. Find that person and ask them. Secretarial staff often know. If the information has costs associated with it, then financial controllers may know.

Model answers

A.   From the public and other corporate bodies.

B.   Generated by the CE's office.

C.   Generated internally from (a) the management reports from the Revenue Collection department (asset # 007.X), (b) the expert judgement of this audit area, and (c) historical economic data from the economics department (asset # 213.1).

WHAT IS THE CURRENT LEVEL OF QUALITY OF THIS INFORMATION ASSET?

What is this attribute?

It is an objective assessment of the quality of the information asset. The criterion of quality is its fitness for its purpose, as judged by the user of the information.

Why does this attribute matter? What is the business case?

Poor quality information can damage the value of an organization in the way that poor quality food can damage the health of a person.

The audit forces the information asset owner to make an assessment of its quality. If there is some junior employee who has been trying to express concerns about the quality of an information asset unsuccessfully for some time, then the information audit is a channel through which their concerns can be communicated quickly and effectively, and also investigated to see whether they have substance.

How should the question be answered?

The auditor should pick one of the following grades:

5 - no quality improvement necessary at all; OR the question is not applicable to this asset (e.g. in the case of a set of emails created within the audit area);

4 - minor improvement in quality necessary, but the cost of living with the existing quality level is < 5% of the audit area's budget;

3 - cost of existing quality of information > 5% of

the audit area's budget but is not a priority given other issues;

2 - quality shortfalls are a major risk to reputation or revenue;

1 -As a result of the information quality problems, the risk of serious injury or death to at least one person is likely.

Tips for answering this question usefully

If in doubt, apply the lowest of the markings that you consider possible.

When not to use this attribute

This attribute should always be used.

Frequently asked questions

How is it possible to be objective? Isn't quality always subjective?

In the sense that someone is being asked to make a judgement call, this could be said to be subjective, but the idea there is better described as a problem of uncertainty or of it being impossible to make a precise quantification. A professional employee should be able to suspend their own personal interests and make an objective assessment of quality; and the way that this attribute is ranked, by respect to the cost consequences of poor quality with respect to human life or, less severely, the budget of the audit area, makes this task easier.

WHAT INDEX OR SEARCH CAPABILITY IS THERE?

What is this attribute?

This attribute records how an information asset is indexed or how it can be searched, if indeed it can be.

Why does this attribute matter? What is the business case?

Information is only worth having if it can be used, and where there is more than the smallest amount of information, the problem is finding it.

How should the question be answered?

Pick the highest ranking that applies to the index or search capability:

5 - search meets operational and FOI/DPA/EIR requirements in full most of the time.

4 - meets operational requirements most of the time but not FOI / DPA/EIR requirements.

3 - meets operational requirements some of the time.

2 - there are material problems with the search capability for operational purposes.

1 - there is no search capability.

Tips for answering this question usefully

Use the search facility to test the answer. Don't just take somebody else's word for it. Say "Show me."

122

When not to use this attribute

This attribute should always be answered.

Frequently asked questions

But we don't need to search it, we know how to get what we want. Why should we bother with this question?

Fine – just record that there is no search capability.

INFORMATION VALUE & RISK

VALUE OF INFORMATION TO THE ORGANIZATION

What is this attribute?

Any asset has value, by definition. All assets have financial value, whatever other value they may have; a painting, for example may be unique and priceless in the aesthetic sense, but at any particular time will have a monetary or financial value which could in principle be established by selling it at auction. In a business or public service organization management must ensure that all assets used are good value for money, or "best value" in the language of the UK public service. We are used to doing this with property and goods and services, and it is exactly the same for information assets, but we are very unused to applying this kind of thinking to information assets.

Rather than try to apply a £ value to an information asset in this attribute, we instead estimate its approximate value relative to the annual budget of the whole organization. This is in fact applying a £ value, albeit an approximate one, but it is an indirect way of doing so and is far less complicated than doing so directly.

Why does this attribute matter? What is the business case?

As we have said, every organization needs to ensure that it manages for value, and this means knowing the value of the assets used in the operations of the organization. Are they being procured cost-effectively? Are there cheaper alternatives? Is the level of stock of an asset

sufficient, deficient or in surplus? Is the asset
being damaged by poor storage? We answer
these vital questions by valuing the asset.

How should the question be answered?

This question is answered on a 1–5 scale that
makes use of the idea of *deprival value*. If we
have the use of an asset and we were suddenly
to be deprived of that asset, how much would
we spend as a direct result of being deprived of
it? This is the key question to establish deprival
value. If we had no need of the asset (which is
to say, strictly speaking, that it was not an asset
at all) then we would spend nothing – we might
even heave a sigh of relief that we no longer had
to worry about it. If we had an urgent, essential
and very great need of the asset, we might spend
a great sum of money to procure an immediate
replacement. Or there is the in-between case
where we would spend some money, but not
that much, because although we need or want
the asset, it would not be filling an urgent or
critical or great need.

The notion of deprival value is so powerful
and so important, let us give colour to the
explanation above with an example. Suppose
that there is a bus depot in which there are
100 buses and two screw turning lathes. The
manager of the depot arrives one Monday
morning and finds that one of the screw turning
lathes has vanished into hyperspace, never to
return. It is the year 2004. Screw turning lathes
cost £5,000 for the cheapest model and £100,000
for the most advanced and high capacity model.
If it is the case that the depot was using both
lathes at full capacity and overtime and was
considering buying a third lathe to cope, then
there is every chance that the manager would

pay £100,000 for the most advanced lathe, and he might even pay extra for same day delivery. At the other extreme, if neither lathe had been being used at all, he would certainly not pay anything for a replacement lathe. Then there are the cases in between. Perhaps one lathe was in fairly full use, with the second being a backup for peak loads or when the first was being maintained; in this case the manager might buy the cheap replacement lathe at £5,000, but would not pay extra for faster delivery. Alternatively, the manager might decide to do without a lathe and enter into an agreement with the neighbouring garage to use its lathe when the depot's was being repaired, at £200 a day. And so on.

In our information audit we use the notion of deprival value as a fraction of the whole organization's annual budget, according to the scale:

5 - The deprival value of this information is greater than 10% of the whole organization's annual budget.

4 - The deprival value of this information is greater than 1% of budget.

3 - Not 5 or 4, but the audit area could not function without this information.

2 - Major expenditure would be necessary if this information was not available. (Major = requires authority beyond that of the manager responsible for the audit area).

1 - Other.

Tips for answering this question usefully
Be realistic.

When not to use this attribute

This attribute should always be used.

Frequently asked questions

Surely no single information asset could have a deprival value of more then 10% of the organization's annual budget? It's only information after all.

Information is an asset like any other – gold, diamonds, people, atomic bombs and hospitals. It can be worth little or much, or anything in between. Were a local council to lose its information on who must pay rates and council tax, it could easily exceed the value of the annual budget: first, there would be no revenue, itself a huge loss of value, then there would be the cost of public enquiries and staff redundancies, which would also be great, and then the cost of re-creating the data from scratch. Impossible? Improbable? Not at all. The UK's Inland Revenue department lost five million records of taxpayers, and the Ministry of Defence was only one paper file away from being unable to provide the effective leadership that it did during the last foot and mouth crisis.

What is an example of a "3"?

A typical example is the press cuttings and personalities file of the Public Relations function. These do not have a deprival value of any great amount, but absent this information there would be little point having a PR function.

COMMENTS ON THE VALUE OF THE INFORMATION ASSET

What is this attribute?

This is the place to record any narrative comments on the value of the asset. For example, what could be done to increase the value or reduce the risk of this asset? Is it information which could be very valuable to others and perhaps sold to them, or should it have special protection from them?

Why does this attribute matter? What is the business case?

If there is a way to increase the value of this information asset to any significant degree, then management should know of it. The information audit is a good way to communicate it.

How should the question be answered?

Narrative text.

Tips for answering this question usefully

Enter only ideas which are likely to have a material impact and which are practicable, feasible and realistic; but if in doubt, record the idea anyway. (Internet was once considered a silly idea by Bill Gates.)

When not to use this attribute

Fill in this attribute only if there is a material idea.

Model answer

This information is collected for health and safety purposes, but could also be used for environmental monitoring, which currently collects similar but different information. There may be reasons why this would not work, but the foreman thinks it is worth investigating.

TIME CRITICALITY

What is this attribute?

How time critical is the information? In other words, how quickly must this information be delivered to its users? The answer depends as much on the business processes in the organization or what the organization does as on the nature of the information. For example, for a holidaymaker off to the beach, the weather forecast is nice to have, but is scarcely time critical. However, for the holidaymaker in his yacht setting off on a sailing expedition who has only six minutes to make the no-return-for-eight-hours trip over the sand-bar at the mouth of the river into the North Sea, the weather information is time critical.

Why does this attribute matter? What is the business case?

Managing information well from the point of view of service delivery is about ensuring that the right information reaches the right person at the right time. We need the menu before the meal, not two hours afterwards; we want to know if the train is going to be late before we rush to the platform missing the chance to buy breakfast, not ten minutes after the advertised departure time (this line of reasoning seems to be a mystery to the First Great Western employee who is nearby as these words are written on a train to Newport, Gwent – and it would be helpful to know also in advance that there is no trolley service due to unforeseen staff shortages.) So, apart from British train companies, in every organization some information will be more time critical than other information. The value of this attribute is to help ensure that information is managed according to its time criticality.

The least time critical information should be archived and the most time critical information should be readily available, whether the information is paper or electronic. Research conducted by Visdalen Corporation of the US in the early 2000's showed that this is a major source of IT cost inefficiency. The research looked at organizations with time critical information. It found that a significant fraction of the average organization's high-availability network storage devices were used to store information that was not particularly time critical, leaving much time critical information in storage which was slower to respond to user needs. In short, with regard to time criticality and availability, the storage available was not aligned to the need for information.

How should the question be answered?

When you need the information asset, how quickly must you obtain it typically?

5 - more than three months

4 - three months

3 - fortnight

2 - day

1 - less than 1 hour

Tips for answering this question usefully

If in doubt between two answers, choose the least time critical.

When not to use this attribute

This attribute should always be used.

BACKUP DATA

What is this attribute?

This attribute records whether there is a backup copy of this information. By this we mean an exact copy that exists specifically for the purpose of disaster recovery backup or business continuity; we do not mean information that is duplicated or duplicated to some extent for other purposes or by chance, which is the subject of the next attribute.

Why does this attribute matter? What is the business case?

Disaster recovery is a key part of information management.

How should the question be answered?

A - Yes, and backups are created automatically by a process controlled by IT or some other function that has specialist expertise in backing up data.

B - Yes, and backups are created automatically but not as per "A".

C - Yes, backups are created by a non-automated but highly controlled process.

D - Yes, backups are created on a regular basis such that it is unlikely more than 5% of this asset would be lost in the event of a disaster.

E - Backups are made on some basis other than above.

F - No backups exist of this data.

Tips for answering this question usefully

Know where the backup is.

Note that paper and microfilm files can be backed up as well as electronic or other digital files.

If there is duplicate data, its location should already be recorded in the corporate disaster recovery plan, but if it is not and you wish to use the information audit to record the location of backup data, then add an extra attribute to the audit template for that purpose. Note that it is not good practice to allow the location of backup data to be widely known, because to do so compromises the security of the backup data.

When not to use this attribute

It may be more efficient to skip this entire column if the organization already has a well-implemented disaster recovery plan. On the other hand, the information audit may be used to audit the completeness and effectiveness of that plan.

What is this attribute?

This attribute shows whether the information in the asset is duplicated in some other information asset and, if so, how it could be eliminated.

Why does this attribute matter? What is the business case?

The rationale for this attribute of the information audit is simply to enable the organization to identify surplus holdings of information. By duplicated we do not mean is there a copy of the information that is held for the purposes of disaster recovery or data backup; we mean any other kind of duplication. The audit assumes that there is backup data of all key information, and in any case that was the subject of the previous attribute.

In the case of physical assets such as stocks of raw materials or plant and equipment, excess holdings are an inefficient use of capital, because the capital is tied up in an asset which is not likely to be used instead of being used for some more productive purpose. The situation with surplus information is similar, but even worse. Like surplus physical assets, surplus information ties up capital unproductively and, like surplus physical assets, it incurs a storage and maintenance cost.

What is worse about redundancy in information assets is that provided a proper disaster recovery plan is in place, and with it the associated backup of the data, there is far less upside to holding surplus information assets than to holding surplus property, plant, equipment and stock. While surplus physical assets may incur great cost and be in some objective way "a bad thing," in real life the objectivity is frequently spurious, and fairly often there is some powerful interest group or individual who has invented an argument about surplus equipment to strip an organization of what is in fact necessary. In this way have many workers lost their pensions, in this way has the British Army lost most of its medical services in the 1990s, and in this way did the Titanic set sail without the lifeboats which would have saved so many lives.

This kind of chicanery on the part of a proportion of the leaders of mankind has probably been going on since time immemorial; the foolish virgins and the prodigal son were not the first to use this line of reasoning, so if we have a natural disposition to think in this way it may be for good reason. But however good a reason it is for thinking that way about the question of redundancy in physical assets, it is not a good reason to think of redundancy in information assets. Physical assets are used up. Once one lifeboat is full of people, another lifeboat is needed if there are more people. It is quite different with information. One song can be copied by any number of people without in any way using up, filling up or exhausting the first copy.

So, assuming always (as we have done in this attribute) that there is a proper backup copy, there is no benefit at all in having duplicate information. There is only cost. Bad enough are the costs of holding the information; mainly space costs in the case of paper information and data storage device costs in the case of digital information. But worse are the costs of reconciling the duplicate copies; where there is a difference between two copies of the same information asset, it is a high cost to resolve differences between them to establish the true information. How do we know there are differences in the first place? We have to check the entire contents of one asset against the other, and that too is expensive.

How should the question be answered?

5 - there is no duplicate information held and this asset is either a golden source or derives from one.

4 - there is definitely no duplicate information, or there is duplicate information but it exists only for the short term and for best practice reasons.

3 - There is duplicate information but not more than 15%.

2 - There is more than 15% duplicate information.

1 - Duplicate and triplicate information exists, duplication is uncontrolled, or duplication is an unmanaged source of reputational or financial or health risk.

Tips for answering this question usefully

The problem with answering this question is that the audit area may not know that other similar or even duplicate information exists. Just do your best!

If there is duplicate data, its location should be given in the earlier attribute, "With what other information assets is this asset closely associated? How?"

When not to use this attribute

This attribute should always be used.

Frequently asked questions

When is information duplicate information and when is it backup data?

As stated above, backup data is data (or an information asset – we use the word "data" because that is the common usage, as in the term "backup data") that has been created specifically as backup data or specifically for the purposes of disaster recovery.

SOURCES OF RISK

What is this attribute?

This attribute records the sources of risk inhering in the information asset, that is the risk from improper disclosure of the information.

Why does this attribute matter? What is the business case?

Risk matters.

How should the question be answered?

Give a short narrative description of the main risks, and if possible some indication of what is judged to be the probability and impact of each.

Tips for answering this question usefully

Think about what would happen if the worst imaginable troublemaker obtained the information, or a competitor, or an opponent in a lawsuit, or a supplier or activist. Remember the quote, "Information is power."

When not to use this attribute

This attribute should always be completed, even if merely to record "No significant risk."

Model answers

A.   The main risk is that a leak of this information could cause severely embarrassing PR, but it would be unlikely to cause long-term damage.

B.   (a) Litigation risk – disgruntled employees would use it.
(b) Reputational risk – it might cost senior management their careers (as in the 1999 case at XYZ.)
(c) Cost risk – we might have to obtain

a different replacement asset, depending on who obtained this one. 50% probability, cost c. £20,000.

C.   No risk.

CUMULATIVE RISK

What is this attribute?

The previous attribute looked at the risk of disclosing an entire information asset. In this attribute, called "cumulative risk," we are concerned only with the special case where elements of a complete asset are released but never the whole asset in one go, which might be the case in some circumstances with the Freedom of Information Act, for example. In this special case there may be a risk that these small, element by element releases of information are collected and re-assembled into a larger component of the information asset, and that the intention was not to release more than a small part of the entire asset may be thwarted. This attribute covers this special type of risk.

Why does this attribute matter? What is the business case?

Risk matters.

How should the question be answered?

If there is a cumulative risk, explain briefly in narrative form why there is.

Tips for answering this question usefully

If this attribute is applicable (see below) to whom would the entire information asset be useful? Why? (e.g. suppliers, customers, protest groups, people who normally have to pay for such information, etc.)

When not to use this attribute

This attribute does not usually apply; it is a special case. Ignore if not applicable.

Model answer

We release individual files from this asset to suppliers in order to assist them in their attempt to supply the organization and to create a fair market. However, we know that many of these suppliers have tried to obtain this information in the past by other means and it is likely that they will try to assemble the entire asset file by file.

INFORMATION LIFECYCLE

ACQUISITION – EVENT DRIVEN OR PERIODIC?

What is this attribute?

Information is created either at regular intervals, or as it is termed in the audit, periodically, or some event that does not occur at regular periods causes it to be created. An example of a periodic creation of information is the annual performance appraisal of a member of staff conducted by a manager. An example of an event- driven creation of information is having to fill in an accident log, because there is no predicting when an accident will happen; accidents do not happen at regular intervals – or so we trust.

Why does this attribute matter? What is the business case?

Whether information is created periodically or as a result of a trigger event matters because it affects the way that information management systems are designed and managed – both the technological and conceptual kind of information management system. One example of the many differences can be that users tend to need to be alerted to an event and its consequent information, whereas users tend to expect periodic information. (At home, most of us expect the newspaper to be delivered; it is a periodic delivery, but we need to be told that there is a parcel to collect; it is an irregular event. For the parcel delivery company, of course, things are different, which shows that whether an information asset's creation or updating is event-driven or periodic is a matter of perspective, but this makes no difference to the different requirements of management systems.)

How should the question be answered?

State either "Event-driven" or "Periodic."

Tips for answering this question usefully

Ask yourself whether this asset is more like a newspaper or more like a parcel – see above.

When not to use this attribute

If you are not certain which term applies to the asset, there is often little harm done if you skip this attribute.

Frequently asked questions

Can an information asset be sometimes periodic and sometimes event- driven?

Yes, in theory: but in practice they tend not to be. If there are many information assets in your organization that appear to be both, then consult your Information Manager or equivalent to verify that this really is the case. If it is, then your organization may wish to drop this attribute from the audit, or to add another possible answer to this attribute, or to agree a protocol for keeping the two possible answers but deciding which one should apply in the in-between case.

RETENTION - HOW OFTEN ARE THE MOST FREQUENTLY ACCESSED 20% OF FILES ACCESSED?

What is this attribute?

This attribute measures how often the most accessed 20% of the asset is in fact accessed.

Why does this attribute matter? What is the business case?

It is possible for there to be an asset where part of the asset is used very often but most of the asset is not used at all. In such a case, to manage the entire asset as if it was all used heavily would be inefficient, for example because instead of archiving most of the asset, which is cheap, it would all be kept at high readiness and high availability, which is expensive.

How should the question be answered?

5 - daily
4 - weekly
3 - monthly
2 - at least once a year
1 - less than once a year

Tips for answering this question usefully

The 20% figure is not intended to be anything but a very rough approximation. If it helps, read the question as omitting the figure, that is "how often are the most frequently accessed 20% of files accessed?"

When not to use this attribute

This attribute may be omitted for small assets or for assets, all parts of which are used to the same degree.

RETENTION - WHAT % OF FILES HAVE BEEN ACCESSED IN THE LAST 3 MONTHS?

What is this attribute?

This attribute is similar to the last, but where the last asked for how often the most frequently used 20% of assets had been used, this asks for what percentage of assets have been used in the last three months.

Why does this attribute matter? What is the business case?

The two attributes taken together - this one and the previous one – will assist in ensuring that the planning of information management is efficient.

How should the question be answered?

As a percentage, to the nearest 10%, rounded up.

Tips for answering this question usefully

An approximate answer is better than no answer provided that the estimate is made by someone who uses the information as a key part of their work, otherwise no estimate is better.

This attribute is most valuable in conjunction with the previous one, or as an alternative to it.

When not to use this attribute

This attribute is one of the more optional ones of the information audit. Ignore it if it is at all problematic to answer.

RETENTION - WHAT SCHEDULE OR REGULATIONS OR POLICY GOVERN DISPOSAL?

What is this attribute?

This attribute lists all rules and regulations that govern how and when the asset may be destroyed.

Why does this attribute matter? What is the business case?

Some information is governed by strict rules about destruction. Enron and its directors and employees are infamous at Enron because that company destroyed information illegally.

How should the question be answered?

Name the document or URL.

Tips for answering this question usefully

If giving the URL then also give the date on which the URL showed the schedule or regulations, as they can change.

When not to use this attribute

This attribute should always be completed.

Frequently asked questions

How can one find out what rules govern the disposal of a particular piece of information?

It ought to be the information owner's responsibility to know this. However, some owners will have been appointed as such only because the audit has identified that the asset had no owner previously, in which case it may be unfair and unreasonable to expect the owner to know immediately. Users of information may know the rules.

Model answers

A.   Caldecott guidelines.

B.   The current (FY 2004-2005) corporate policy is that each record in this asset should be retained until December 31st of the seventh calendar year after its creation, after which date it must be destroyed at the earliest possible opportunity and in any case within three months, unless the information has been requested for the purposes of an enquiry or similar event.

C.   Police & Criminal Evidence Act.

146

DISPOSAL - WHAT MECHANISM ENSURES THAT THE LATEST VERSION OF THESE IS APPLIED?

What is this attribute?

This attribute explains how the rules, listed in the previous attribute, actually get enforced ...

Why does this attribute matter? What is the business case?

... so that management can, in the first place, get a sense of the likelihood that they are being enforced, and, secondly and if necessary, take steps to ensure enforcement of the rules. Just think! If Enron had had an information audit with this attribute it might never have gone bust and its fabulously well-paid employees would have kept their jobs, pay, pensions and reputation!

How should the question be answered?

Give a short narrative description of how the rules listed in the previous attribute are enforced.

Tips for answering this question usefully

A short, relevant answer is more valuable than a long, irrelevant answer.

When not to use this attribute

Where the previous attribute has been completed, so should this one be.

Frequently asked questions

What if one does not know how the rules are enforced?

Then say so.

Model answers

A.   Internal and external audit checks the

enforcement on a regular basis, always more frequently than annually.

B.   Each month a duty officer makes a random inspection of files and signs the confidential file register to attest that any destruction of records has been carried out in accordance with ..., as per Standing Order SHAEF/1066/AAT.

CONTROL AND REPORTING

WHO OWNS THIS INFORMATION ASSET?

What is this attribute?

This attribute names the person or function who owns the information asset.

Why does this attribute matter? What is the business case?

If it is necessary to obtain the information or to find out something about it then it will be valuable to know who is its owner.

How should the question be answered?

Enter their appointment (alternatively known as their post) and telephone extension.

Tips for answering this question usefully

The most useful way to record this attribute is to enter both the post and the name of the individual filling that post, as well as their telephone number. Then if the individual takes up a new post and is uncontactable, there is some clue as to how to find their successor.

When not to use this attribute

This attribute should always be used. Some individuals may be concerned about their privacy if their name is listed here, but in the case of all public sector organizations their name will be a matter of public record (this is a recent development), and having it recorded in the information audit is in the public interest.

Similar arguments apply for private sector information audits.

Model answer

John Rorkes-Drift VC, x 1879, Chief Barricade Officer (CBO), office is at Pietermaritzburg.

150

WHO WITHIN THE AUDIT AREA IS THE CUSTODIAN OF THE ASSET?

What is this attribute?

The previous attribute recorded details of the individual who owns the information asset. In addition to an owner there may be someone who, while not the owner of the asset, is the day to day administrator or custodian of it. This is where their details are recorded.

In all other regards this attribute is the same as the previous one.

IS THIS ASSET SUBJECT TO DPA, EIR, FOI OR THE OGCP?

What is this attribute?

This attribute lists the main disclosure statutes which apply to the asset or parts of it.

Why does this attribute matter? What is the business case?

This attribute helps to ensure that the organization complies with the relevant statutes quickly and efficiently.

How should the question be answered?

List all which apply of FOI, EIR, DPA and OGCP.

Tips for answering this question usefully

The list FOI, EIR, DPA and OGCP applies only to public sector bodies and other bodies subject to FOI. Private sector bodies in the UK are subject to DPA and may wish either to curtail the list of options in this attribute to solely DPA, or may wish to add to DPA other disclosure requirements which govern them. In the case of financial institutions this may include various Financial Services Authority (FSA) regulations on disclosing information, and in the case of corporations with shares traded on public markets in the USA, it may include the Sarbanes-Oxley Act.

When not to use this attribute

This attribute should always be used. If there is any doubt about whether one of the statutes applies to a particular information asset, seek advice from your line manager, or if they are unable to help, via them from either the in-house legal services department or general counsel, or from the corporate information officer.

SHOULD THE INFORMATION BE EXEMPT FROM DISCLOSURE UNDER FOI?

What is this attribute?

This attribute records the opinion of either the information owner or the audit area on whether the information should, as a rule, be exempt from disclosure under FOI.

Why does this attribute matter? What is the business case?

The presumption under FOI is that an information asset should be disclosed. However, there are many and complicated exemptions from the duty to disclose, and for good reason, but unless someone flags up that there is a case for non-disclosure, there is a great risk that the information will be disclosed. This attribute is a mechanism and communication channel to manage that risk.

How should the question be answered?

Enter either "Yes" (that is it is felt that the information should be exempt from disclosure under FOI) or "No."

When not to use this attribute

This attribute is relevant only to public authorities and other organizations that are subject to the Freedom of Information Act.

IF THE INFORMATION SHOULD BE EXEMPT FROM DISCLOSURE UNDER FOI, SAY WHY.

What is this attribute?

This attribute is a narrative explanation for the 'yes' or 'no' opinion given in the previous attribute.

Why does this attribute matter? What is the business case?

The case is the same as for the previous attribute

How should the question be answered?

Give the reason why it is felt that the information should not be disclosed under FOI, in narrative form.

Tips for answering this question usefully

Give a narrative description of the opinion. If possible, state the particular exemption or exemptions that are felt to apply.

When not to use this attribute

As with the previous attribute, this attribute is relevant only to public authorities and other organizations that are subject to the Freedom of Information Act.

Model answers

A.   To release this information would compromise our ability to negotiate fair prices with suppliers, who are usually in a near-monopoly position. This is the balance of public interest exemption.

B.   This information relates to criminal investigations in progress, which is a specific exemption under FOI.

B. This information asset contains much
    personal data, which is exempt from FOI but
    covered by the DPA. Heavy redaction will be
    necessary before disclosure.

IS THIS ASSET IN THE PUBLICATION SCHEME? IF NOT, SHOULD IT BE?

What is this attribute?

This attribute records whether the information asset is in the publication scheme and, if it is not, whether it should be.

Why does this attribute matter? What is the business case?

This attribute helps to ensure that all documents are in the publication scheme of the organization that are required to be and ensures FOI compliance.

How should the question be answered?

Enter "Yes, it is in the scheme" if it is, enter "No, it is not but should be" if it is not but should be, or enter "No, it is not and should not be" if it is not and should not be.

Tips for answering this question usefully

Check the publication scheme of the organization and see if the information falls into one of the classes of material listed.

When not to use this attribute

This attribute is relevant only to public authorities and other organizations that are subject to the Freedom of Information Act.

Frequently asked questions

Q. *Where can I find the publication scheme?*

Model answer

A. On the organization's intranet or web site. Also, the reception should have paper copies.

WHY (SHOULD IT BE / NOT BE) IN THE PUBLICATION SCHEME?

What is this attribute?

This attribute describes the decision made in the previous attribute.

Why does this attribute matter? What is the business case?

The case is the same for the previous attribute.

How should the question be answered?

Give the reason why it is felt that the information should/should not be in the publication scheme. Examples of suitable answers include:

"This asset should be in the publication scheme as it is in one of the classes of the publication scheme."

"This asset should be in the publication scheme as it is information that we make available to the public on a regular basis."

"This asset should not be in the publication scheme as it contains personal information that is exempt from disclosure under the Data Protection Act exemption of the Freedom of Information Act."

"This asset should not be in the publication scheme as it contains information of a confidential nature"

"This asset should not be in the publication scheme as it contains information that is not made available to the public on a regular basis."

Tips for answering this question usefully

Give a narrative description of the opinion.

When not to use this attribute

This attribute is relevant only to public authorities and other organizations that are subject to the Freedom of Information Act.

Frequently asked questions

> Q. *What is held in the publication scheme?*

Model answer

> A. Information that the public authority intends to publish on a regular basis.

WHAT STANDARDS AND REGULATIONS MUST BE APPLIED (ARE MANDATORY) TO THIS ASSET?

What is this attribute?

This attribute describes the quality standards and rules governing this information asset.

Why does this attribute matter? What is the business case?

This attribute helps to ensure that the organization complies with the relevant standards and regulations quickly and efficiently.

How should the question be answered?

All standards and regulations applying to the asset must be listed, including those relating to the quality of the information. Examples of which include:

BS ISO 15489 - Information and documentation
BS ISO 12653 - Electronic imaging
BS EN 8204 - Document management
DD ENV 13606 - Health informatics. Electronic healthcare records
KIT 93 - Records management
PAS 2001:2001 - Knowledge management

The Pensions Schemes (Provision of Information) Regulations 2004
The Radiation (Emergency Preparedness and Public Information) Regulations 2001
The Environmental Information Regulations 1992
Disclosure of Confidential Information Regulations 2001
Police and Criminal Evidence Act 1984

Tips for answering this question usefully

List all relevant standards and regulations that

apply to this asset and, where possible, the section of those standards and regulations.

When not to use this attribute

This attribute should always be used. If there is any doubt about whether one of the statutes applies to a particular information asset, seek advice from your line manager, or if they are unable to help, via them from either the in-house legal services department or general counsel, or from the corporate information officer.

WHAT IS THE CATEGORY IN THE LOCAL GOVERNMENT CATEGORY LIST FOR THIS INFORMATION ASSET?

What is this attribute?

This asset describes the category in the Local Government Category List for this information asset.

Why does this attribute matter? What is the business case?

The Local Government Category List provides a controlled vocabulary for local government and community resources categorised in a hierarchical structure.

How should the question be answered?

This question should be answered by using one of the top-level headings given below:

- Business
- Community and living
- Council, government and democracy
- Education and learning
- Environment
- Health and social care
- Housing
- Jobs and careers
- Legal services
- Leisure and culture
- Policing and public safety
- Social issues
- Transport and streets

Tips for answering this question usefully

A good answer is one that describes the asset within the terms of the Local Government Category List, using the top level categories given above.

When not to use this attribute

This attribute is relevant only to public authorities and other organizations that are subject to the Freedom of Information Act.

Frequently asked questions

There are many categories that this asset may be described by, how do I know which one to choose?

Model answer

Seek advice from your line manager, or if they are unable to help, via them from either the in-house legal services department or general counsel, or from the corporate information officer.

WHAT E-GOVERNMENT METADATA STANDARD APPLIES TO THIS INFORMATION ASSET?

What is this attribute?

The e-Government Metadata Standard provides the coding schemes to be used by government officers when creating metadata for their information resources or when designing systems for information systems.

Why does this attribute matter? What is the business case?

The e-Government Metadata Standard is required by Government to enable consistency of metadata across public sector organizations. Additionally, the e-Government Metadata Standard is a part of the e-Government Interoperability Framework (e-GIF).

How should the question be answered?

By listing the elements of the metadata standards that apply to the asset. The elements provided by the Office of the e-Envoy are as follows:

- Accessibility
- Addressee
- Aggregation
- Audience
- Contributor
- Coverage
- Creator
- Date
- Description
- Digital Signature
- Disposal
- Format
- Identifier

- Language
- Location
- Mandate
- Preservation
- Publisher
- Relation
- Rights
- Source
- Status
- Subject
- Title
- Type

Tips for answering this question usefully

Use the metadata standards as provided by the e-Envoy, http://www.govtalk.gov.uk/ schemasstandards/metadata.asp

Frequently asked questions

What metadata standard do I apply?

Model answer

Use a standard that you believe best describes the asset; if unable to do so seek advice from your line manager or from the corporate information officer.

164

WHAT DISCRETIONARY STANDARDS ARE APPLIED TO THIS ASSET?

What is this attribute?

This attribute describes the discretionary standards are applied to this asset.

Why does this attribute matter? What is the business case?

This records any discretionary standards are applied to this asset.

How should the question be answered?

By listing all discretionary standards are applied to this asset. These will include:

- Information storage policies
- Document destruction policies
- Document retention policies

Tips for answering this question usefully

Obtain details of the discretionary standards used in the organization.

When not to use this attribute

If there are no discretionary standards used in the organization.

Frequently asked questions

What discretionary standards are applied to this asset?

Model answer

Seek advice from your line manager or from the corporate information officer.

MUST THIS INFORMATION BE KEPT FOR AUDIT OR COMPLIANCE PURPOSES?

What is this attribute?

This attribute describes whether this asset must be kept for audit or compliance purposes.

Why does this attribute matter? What is the business case?

This attribute helps the organization comply with relevant audits or compliance issues quickly and efficiently.

How should the question be answered?

Answer "Yes" if the asset is required for audit or compliance purposes.

Answer "No" if the asset is not required for audit or compliance purposes.

Answer "in part" if some of the asset is required for audit or compliance purposes.

When not to use this attribute

This attribute must always be used.

Frequently asked questions

What audit or compliance purposes may this asset be required for?

Model answer

Seek advice from your line manager or from the corporate information officer.

IS THIS ASSET USED AS A MAJOR COMPONENT IN MANAGEMENT REPORTING?

What is this attribute?

This attribute describes whether this asset is used as a major component in management reporting.

Why does this attribute matter? What is the business case?

This is important to the running of the organization, as incomplete reporting may leave the organization in breach of various legislations.

How should the question be answered?

Answer "Yes" if this asset is used as a major component in management reporting.

Answer "No" if this asset is not used as a major component in management reporting.

Tips for answering this question usefully

Also answer "Yes" if this information is mandated in the mission statement or terms of reference of the audit area.

When not to use this attribute

Always use this attribute.

Frequently asked questions

What is the mission statement or terms of reference of the audit area?

Model answer

You line manager should be able to provide you with this information.

FOR INFORMATION OWNED BY THE AUDIT AREA, WITH WHOM ELSE DO YOU SHARE INFORMATION?

What is this attribute?

This attribute describes with whom else this asset is shared with externally to the organisation.

Why does this attribute matter? What is the business case?

This attribute enables the organization to identify which information assets are being shared externally.

How should the question be answered?

The name of the external party with whom the information is shard should be entered. Examples include:

- The CPS
- Partnership organisations
- The local Police Force
- The Local NHS Trust
- The Local Council
- Government Departments
- PFI partners
- Local pressure groups

Tips for answering this question usefully

Give contact details for the external party.

When not to use this attribute

Always use this attribute.

FOR INFORMATION OWNED BY THE AUDIT AREA, WHAT IS THE COST TO YOU OF SHARING THIS INFORMATION?

What is this attribute?

This attribute records the cost of sharing the asset with an external party.

Why does this attribute matter? What is the business case?

This enables the organization to be able to understand the cost of sharing information externally.

How should the question be answered?

Answer "High" if more than 5% of the audit area's time is spent administering the sharing of information, or sharing creates risks which are not currently managed and which could materially impact the reputation or functioning of the audit area or the organization as a whole.

Answer "Medium" if a noticeable part of the audit area's time is spent administering the sharing of information, or material (but less than high) risks are caused by having to share the information.

Answer "Low" for anything else.

When not to use this attribute

Only use this attribute if information is being shared externally, i.e., do not use this attribute if the information is not shared externally to the organization.

WHO ARE THE INTERNAL (WITHIN AUDIT AREA) USERS, BY FUNCTION?

What is this attribute?

This attribute records who within the audit area uses the asset.

Why does this attribute matter? What is the business case?

This attribute allows the organization to know who is using the information within the audit area.

How should the question be answered?

Listing the names of the users within the audit area. e.g.:
Jo Bloggs, Administrator, extension 1234.

Tips for answering this question usefully

If possible, give the role of the user in addition to their full name.

When not to use this attribute

This attribute must always be used.

EXTERNAL TO THE AUDIT AREA, WHO USES THE INFORMATION?

What is this attribute?

This attribute records who within the organisation, but external to the audit area, uses this asset.

Why does this attribute matter? What is the business case?

This case is the same for the previous attribute.

How should the question be answered?

Listing the names of the users external to the audit area, but internal to the organisation, e.g.: Jo Bloggs, Administrator, Administration Department extension 1234.

Tips for answering this question usefully

This case is the same for the previous attribute.

When not to use this attribute

This attribute must always be used.

Appendix A

THE UK's FREEDOM OF INFORMATION ACTS AND INFORMATION AUDIT

The Freedom of Information Act can be seen
in the general context of disclosure legislation.
In the UK, the best-known existing disclosure
legislation is the Data Protection Act, which
gives individuals the right to obtain information
held about them, the right to have that
information corrected, and the right to prevent
improper use of that information. Other laws
and practices that comprise what is becoming
known as the 'access to information' or 'A2I'
movement include:

- Parliamentary questions (UK and old
  Commonwealth),
- Environmental information regulations (UK),
- Sarbanes Oxley Act (USA),
- Local government Code of Practice, (UK).

The UK is the last of the major English-speaking
countries to enact a freedom of information law.
The US, Canada, Australia, New Zealand and
the Republic of Ireland have all had this law
for some time, as have a number of European
countries.

There are two main reasons for the increase in
access to information legislation and practices.
One is that an increasing number of citizens
want this; citizens are demanding this right in

order to ensure good governance, to identify irresponsible behaviour early, and to ensure that the state and corporations comply with their duties and meet their promises. Another is the development of information technology.

IT has had three notable ramifications for access to information, and together these further increase the demand for access to information. First, information technology has increased the amount of information held, so there is more to see. Secondly, IT makes it practicable to provide access to information, by reducing the cost and effort of doing so. And thirdly, IT increases the risk, or at least the perceived risk, that governments and organizations will abuse the power which holding information gives them.

These reasons derive from both major and permanent trends. This means that the access to information movement is going to continue, and it is also going to grow. We believe that the access to information market will grow for at least 20 years as the importance of access to information is recognised more and more widely and as continued advances in IT increase its importance and reduce the barriers to managing information.

THE FREEDOM OF INFORMATION ACT

The Freedom of Information Act applies to England, Wales and Northern Ireland. A similar Act applies in Scotland. The Acts apply to all public authorities and some companies. The government department which owns the Act is the Department for Constitutional Affairs, formerly the Lord Chancellor's Department. The

Information Commissioner enforces compliance with the Act. (Slightly different arrangements exist in Scotland.)

The two essential obligations of the Act are:

1.   To produce a publication scheme, in effect a menu of information that is published as a matter of course, and for other information;

2.   To confirm or deny whether information requested exists and, subject to certain exemptions, to provide a copy of the information.

Even if information is exempt from disclosure, the public authority must still locate the information, not least so that it can read it to justify the exemption. If on the other hand the information does not exist, then the authority must be certain that it does not. Where information is exempt the authority will usually be required to provide copies of the document but with the exempted information blacked out or redacted. (Redacted is a technical term and means edited). Whenever information is withheld the authority must keep a record of its reasons for exempting the information, and of course these must be lawful reasons. Embarrassment is not of itself such a reason.

The obligations imposed by the Act are onerous and disruptive for public authorities. Some parts of the UK public service may have to change their attitudes to disclosing information – as the TV show *Yes, Minister* had it, "You can have government or you can be open." The cultural change required by the Act will be very great.

WHAT FREEDOM OF INFORMATION WILL MEAN

Under FOI anyone will be able to request any information from any public body in the UK. Public bodies have the duty to confirm or deny that they possess that information and to disclose it to the applicant. If an exemption applies, they must explain so to the applicant. Therefore, the exemption processes must be documented, either the disclosure or the appraisal, since a dissatisfied applicant may appeal to the Information Commissioner.

The UK Acts are very similar to FOI Acts in other jurisdictions, but are the most demanding of any such legislation. The UK has incorporated into its own FOI Acts the lessons learnt in other FOI jurisdictions to be the enforcement regime in the UK, which is more effective than in any other jurisdiction. The UK Act is enforced in the first instance not by the courts, which would increase costs to the ordinary citizen, but by the Information Commissioner, who also administers the Data Protection Act. The Commissioner has formal powers, including the power to enter premises and seize documents.

The purpose in this Appendix is to describe how FOI creates a need for information audit rather than to go into details of the Act[1]. It is those features of the Act which create the need for Information Audit which have been described here.

THE SECTION 46 CODE OF PRACTICE TO

THE ACT

All public bodies need to perform an information audit because it is a recommendation in the s46 Code of Practice. (The exact wording of the Code of Practice to the Act – s. 8.4 – is "information survey or record audit" but we have simplified this with the term "information audit"). As a recommendation it falls short of being a statutory requirement, but there are two reasons for public bodies to implement the recommendation. First, it is clearly the intention that public authorities should do so, and any public authority which fails to do so will be increasing its reputational risks under the Act significantly. And secondly, it is hard to see how an Authority could meet the obligations of the other than by conducting an information audit.

The s46 Code of Practice makes the following three recommendations in relation to an information audit:

"… allow employees and their successors to undertake appropriate actions … to facilitate an audit of the business by anyone so authorised." (8.2)

Arrange its records in such a way "that will enable the authority to obtain the maximum benefit from the quick and easy retrieval of information." (8.3)

"A prerequisite for achieving effective records-keeping systems is the information survey or record audit. This gives an objective view of an authority's records and their relationship to organizational functions …." (8.4)

The Act does not say in any detail what an information audit is. The Melbourne information audit, the subject of this book, has been designed to meet the requirements of the Act and was designed in working with many public authorities during their preparations for freedom of information. Information management practices are at the heart of freedom of information compliance, as made explicit in the Section 46 Code of Practice:

"Freedom of information legislation requires that electronic records be managed consistently within regulatory frameworks."

"Effective electronic records management supports administration of data protection principles and effective implementation of freedom of information ... through good organization of records."

Note that while the s46 Code of Practice specifies an information audit, it states explicitly that the reason for requiring effective records management is to arrange its records in such a way "that will enable the authority to obtain the maximum benefit from the quick and easy retrieval of information." The Code of Practice is implying that an information audit should be done in order to increase the efficiency and effectiveness in retrieving information. The Melbourne information audit described in this book is designed to do precisely this.

---

1   For a commentary on the Act see *Blackstone's Guide to the Freedom of Information Act 2000*, Wadham, J. *et al.*, London (Blackstone Press): 2001. ISBN 1-84174-172-8.